You and a Narcissist
100 Mantras
for maintaining
YOUR PEACE amid THEIR CHAOS

By

Kimberly Harding, PhD

For all those having to relate and engage with a narcissist in their lives:

You know who you are.
You can not be responsible for crazy.
You can, however, be responsible to yourself.
May you find calm within the storm.

For all those narcissists who may chance upon this book:

You never know who you are.
This book, like everything else in your life, is all about you.
But like your ironic relationship with mirrors, you will never recognize yourself within it.

"The Queen's Conundrum"

Here we have an image of the Narcissistic Queen on her throne.
She speaks of love. In fact, in her mind, she is all about love.
Don't you notice her heart-shaped chair and face?

The fact her eyes are blanked out "X's" should not concern you.
Of course, she sees you. Really, she does.
It is just that she can't be bothered to open her eyes and actually look at you.

She prefers the peaceful darkness of fantasy
to which closed eyes are a necessity.

Please note her crown hovering overhead,
an ever-present signal of her status and authority.
Whether she has done anything to warrant these trappings does not matter.
Her crown is there, and in her mind, she deserves it.

Sigh. She is waiting.
Upon her throne. Upon her throne of love.
Waiting. Bored? A little.

Everyone who has ever loved her has failed her completely.
Now she must wait.
to see how you shall love (fail) her today.

For she is, after all, the Queen of the Narcissists, "loved" by all.

Drawing the Lines

If you picked up this book, you most likely have a specific purpose in mind.

Before proceeding, I want to make certain you understand who I am and how this material may or may not resonate with you.

I am not a trained psychologist or mental health professional. My doctoral degree is in the biological sciences.

I have read that some in the mental health field dislike untrained individuals "diagnosing" others or using terms such as "narcissism". This is understandable. You likely work in a profession with its own vocabulary as well.

Being untrained in a field, though, does not mean we can not relate to a term. Those people with a narcissist in their lives (as they choose to define this individual) appear to share strikingly similar experiences.

If you have dealt with a narcissist, you know the language before it is spoken. You know the story before it has been told, no matter your educational background. Narcissism is not an issue of semantics for you, for you have lived it.

Although this book discusses typical narcissistic behaviors, the book is not about the narcissist, but rather it is for you, the one attempting to find firm ground amid narcissistic chaos.

Why Mantras?

I use mantras all the time.   In fact, I listen to mantras so often while driving that I refer to my car as the "Mantra Mobile".

All of the mantras I listen to are not in English. Most of them, in fact, are not. But that does not lessen the energetic impact of a few chosen words of awareness repeated and imprinted on our minds and souls.

Mantras help recalibrate the mind and spirit, and if you are interacting with a narcissist, recalibration is essential.

As I have interacted with a few narcissists in my life, I found myself creating mantras to help me understand and find my power within this harmful dynamic.   (Any time you interact with a narcissist, it is harmful.)

In this book, I cover a number of behaviors and situations that arise when a narcissist is present. At the end of each topic is a mantra designed to counteract the instability that may be engendered by narcissists.

You are welcome to read the book in order or each page as a standalone entry.

I hope the mantras keep your feet firmly on the ground and your head and spirit clear, as you deal with one of the most challenging of relationships.

Warning

Abuse and trauma occur on all levels. The mantras are designed to help clarify your thinking, but your safety comes first.
When your safety, or those you love, is at risk- SEEK HELP.
Surviving Narcissism 101 begins with the awareness that
YOU MATTER.
Make certain to align your actions with this understanding.

Ode to the Narcissist

Oh, my sweet, sweet narcissist
Look at you-
In your graceless sorrow and sorrowful greatness
Preening as if all the world was but a stage

Head and neck extended, attempting as you do, to relate.
The plaintive, sick warble issues from your throat
"I can not see. I can not see."

"What would there be to see?" asks I, standing idly by

You turn, teeth exposed,
Raven-ous in your devouring blackness
Nuance is never your strong point, while rage is your default

"I know your little secret," I whisper in conspiracy

Paintings capture your vision -locked unto that pool-
You have stood by that damn pool for eons, Searching

Only now I know- It's not the reflection which drives
your intent and fires your motivation
but rather, the secret we now share

You are staring because you see nothing but your own blackness
and
You are hoping and
You are praying

If you stare long enough
If you stare hard enough

You will see yourself

As Echo and witness to your ever-lasting gaze
I simply say, "I wish you luck"

And those four words almost kill you.

The Power of the Echo

With narcissism, there is always more to the story.

One of the most familiar images of narcissism is of Narcissus, the young man enamored with his reflection, gazing into a pool. Often overlooked is the character depicted next to him, that of Echo.

In the myth, Echo falls in love with Narcissus, and as her name implies, she has no voice of her own.

A witness without a voice is an apt description of what it is to live with a narcissist. So many of us have served as Echo to the narcissist and in time have grown tired, thankfully, of this secondary role.

Yet, this role of being the Echo to the narcissist's self-gazing has always carried a bit of power along with it.

The myth has us believing that Narcissus is caught up staring at his "wonderful" reflection.

As you have likely learned, though, narcissists stare and stare at their reflection, hoping to find something authentic. When they can not find self-reflection, they turn to you, the Echo.

The Echo is expected, along with everyone else in the narcissist's life, to create what the narcissist can not- a sense of self.

This is why narcissists are such needy people. They need you to create for them, through your reflection of them. Without you, they are nothing.

I am much too beautiful and wonderful to serve as someone's Echo.

You don't Know

Narcissists insist that you do not know what you know.

Explaining a narcissist to someone who has never lived with or attempted to relate to one is difficult. Sometimes when I talk to people about narcissism, all I can think is "You don't know…"

"You don't know" what it is like to hear someone tell you one thing, yet mean something entirely different, while you are to act as if you do not notice the difference.

"You don't know" what it is like to be told story after story after story that looks great on the surface, while you both "see" and "un-see" the underpinnings holding that story together.

"You don't know" what it is like to see reality and have to adjust your perception to survive.

"You don't know" what it is like to see it all and have to tell nothing.

"You don't know" what it is like to witness every sick manipulation in the book and be expected to participate as if it were all "understandable".

"You don't know" what it is like to be expected to live out a narrative that you know has no basis in reality.

"You don't know" what it is like to carry the weight of telling lies to yourself so that another may live his or her lie-filled "truth".

If you live with a narcissist or must interact with one, you do know. Don't tell yourself that you don't.

I know the truth.

Cleaning the Mirror

Narcissists do not self-reflect; they project.

Narcissists are beautifully represented, of course, by the fairy tale snippet of "Mirror, Mirror on the wall, who is the fairest of them all?" which serves as the narcissistic motto.

But, like most things dealing with narcissists, this idea is multi-faceted.

If narcissistic craziness was limited to delusional, self-aggrandizing self-reflection, it would be one thing. It is quite another when the poor reflective capabilities of the narcissist are extended to everyone.

Narcissists induce a sense of destabilization by distorting the self-reflections of all around them.

The narcissist works hard to make certain you are not aware of who you are. The narcissist dirties, cracks, smudges and breaks your symbolic self-reflective mirror in order to keep control of you.

You waste a great deal of energy trying to "fix" yourself. But, you are not "fixing" yourself. You are attempting to "fix" the narcissist's distorted perception and projection of you.

Stop gazing in the narcissist's broken, cracked, and projected view of you and clean up our own self-reflection.

I am powerful enough to create and maintain honest self-reflection, apart from the distorted projections of others.

A Stich in Time

A stitch in time is a wasted stitch with a narcissist.

Someone close to me used to say, "A stitch in time saves nine", meaning to address a problem immediately, when it is still small.

Obviously, the person who created this saying never had to interact with a narcissist. A stitch in time saves little to nothing with a narcissist.

Holes always need repair in the life of a narcissist. Whether it is finances, poor work performances, or family dynamics, narcissists are so limited developmentally, it is impossible for there not to be gaps.

In the effort to save time and energy, you may symbolically place a stitch to shore up and repair these openings. And right behind you, stitch for stitch, the narcissist pulls apart the repairs.

You get the finances under control and the narcissist spends more. You fix the family rift, and the narcissist makes a comment to rip it wide open.

You place the symbolic stitch, the narcissist removes it. You place the stitch, the narcissist removes it. When your best efforts are undermined right in front of your face, a sense of despondency may develop.

You can not control a narcissist. You can, however, control how you feel about your actions.

If you place an appropriate, timely stitch and the narcissist rips it out, don't despair. You made the choice to attempt a repair. You can choose to do the same again or not. The power always resides in knowing the choice is yours.

Awareness and insights are mine. Although they may not heal the problem, they heal me.

The Learning Curve

The learning curve for a narcissist plateaued some time ago.

I have found that rather than learning and growing over time, narcissists simply refine their techniques of control.

Narcissists can be excellent teachers, though. Although, I would never suggest any one voluntarily sign up for their program.

When you are with a narcissist, you learn lessons you never desired. You learn lessons you never dreamed of having. You learn lessons you never imagined. And you learn lessons that you never once thought someone would long to teach you.

But, you do learn.

Maybe not the lessons you hoped for, but to survive dealing with a narcissist, you must be able to learn, and learn you do.

You learn. A narcissist does not. And that makes all the difference.

My ability to learn and grow is endless.

The Telemarketer Approach

In their demanding conversational style, narcissists can be as clueless and aggressive as some telemarketers.

Narcissists sometimes converse with you much like a telemarketer would. They are more interested in their scripted agenda than they are in you. Unless a two-way conversation has something in it for them, they really are not that interested.

In this way, you can turn the tables on the narcissist.

If he or she is going to speak AT you, rather than converse WITH you, well, then perhaps you should treat the narcissist with the same time and attention you do a telemarketer.

I learned this idea from overhearing one man handle a phone call from a narcissist. As I was in the room with this person, I saw him continue on with his activity, giving little attention to the call, other than a murmured, "Yep", "Uh-huh", and "Sounds good". When I asked what the call was about, he stated, "I don't know. You know her. She is always rambling."

Rather than getting emotionally excited about the narcissist's ramblings, this man had managed to maintain a steady balance. Not always an easy thing to do.

You can not always check out on a narcissist in this manner. However, sometimes responding to the narcissist with the same energy and focus as you would a telemarketer is a great strategy.

It saves time and emotional energy. It also makes you realize that narcissists, although they like to be front and center in everyone's life, may not have anything important to say. And sometimes, the best response is to simply hang up.

I choose the amount of energy I want to expend.

Banished

Disagreeing with a narcissist's view is the quickest way to get yourself banished from the kingdom.

Narcissists are territorial when it comes to "reality". They protect their version of reality as if they were in a life and death battle. Sometimes you may find yourself in such a fight with a narcissist, thinking, "What's the big deal? This is just a small point of disagreement."

Not. To. The. Narcissist.

One toe out of the kingdom boundary by you is seen as an act of treason by the narcissist.

Why? The narcissist has so much at risk.

If any significant person in the narcissist's sphere of control begins to poke holes in the narcissist's self-created world, the narcissist believes everything is lost.

Having so little potential for authentic existence, the narcissist depends on others to keep his or her world vision afloat. Poke too many holes in it, and the narcissist worries it will sink.

If you become too forthright in your accusations (or even kind statements) that the narcissist's reality may be a little off- you are either dismissed from the narcissist's world completely or brought back under full control immediately.

Narcissists need you much more than you need them, simply because they depend on you to keep their vision.

Disagreements are a normal part of life. I do not have to let others control me through this aspect.

Species

What is the rarest type of narcissist? A happy one.

A happy, joyous narcissist is a creature of myths and fables, like the ever-elusive unicorn.

Narcissists can be manic.
Narcissists can be cruel.
Narcissists can be clueless.

But happy and joyous? Not so much.

The only time I see narcissists with a sense of "humor" is when they witness someone else suffering. They find pleasure in that, but not much else.

And this is where you are let off the hook.

You can not make narcissists happy, despite their demanding that you try.

The narcissist's brain short-circuited somewhere along the line, and the neuronal path to happiness was circumvented. It is not up to you to reroute this path or find a detour.

Do we wish everyone could be happy? Sure we do....but that does not mean the responsibility is on you.

You have not failed the narcissist in any way. The capacity for joy and happiness is not something you can give someone.

I am only responsible for my own happiness.

Always the Victim

Narcissists, in their own minds, are always the victim, never the bride.

No matter what the situation, narcissists always feel left out and victimized. I have witnessed entire events, such as someone's wedding, be derailed by a narcissist who did not feel "enough" special attention was being paid to him or her.

To the narcissist, it is irrelevant who the day is "supposed" to be about. The narcissist may, technically, be a superficial figure. In a narcissist's mind, the event should still, somehow, significantly include him or her.

Narcissists are excellent at manipulating not just individuals, but entire groups. Some groups even assign someone to monitor the narcissist in the hopes that this person, with complete focus on the narcissist, can anticipate and circumvent any narcissistic melt-down.

If you have been around narcissists enough, though, you know the narcissist eventually rears his or her ugly head, creating a mess of everything and placing all the attention on him or her.

As all eyes turn on them, are these narcissists now happy and fulfilled? No. They are still angry, hurt, and vengeful. They play the sympathy card, wanting everyone to see them as the "victim". In the meantime, they do everything possible to be the "bride", getting front and center attention.

For any special event or occasion, understand the purpose. Focus on what and how you want to celebrate. If the narcissist is unable to handle the event, well, perhaps, the narcissist should not be invited.

I honor the purpose and meaning that special occasions and celebrations hold for me.

Psyche Fatigue Fracture

Narcissists create the tiny cracks that eventually result in the shattering.

On some days, you are surprised how your buttons can be pushed. After years of interacting with a narcissist, you may find yourself in tears or throwing an object against the wall over some small issue.

I call this response a "psyche fatigue fracture".

In physics, the concept of fatigue refers to the wearing down of a material by repetitive loads. The loads need not be large to cause damage, as it is the culmination of repetitions that weakens the material.

The same thing happens when repetitive loads are applied to your psyche. Narcissists constantly bombard us with their needs, wants, desires, anger, frustration, and chaos. Each of these individually can be handled. However, over time, we get worn down, and eventually a crack or two manifests.

The best approach to handling a fatigue fracture of the psyche is to understand what is happening, and as much as possible, get the narcissistic load off of you.

When cracks in the psyche develop, see them as signs of fatigue and that you need to take a break. Don't tell yourself that the demands and behaviors of the narcissist are "no big deal". Individual acts may not be. Cumulatively, however, they are a burdensome weight.

Remember, the narcissist can not change, so you must. Take the breaks that your psyche needs. Treat YOURSELF well and heal your own cracks. You did not make them, but you can heal them.

My capacity to regenerate is infinite.

Here...but no farther...

In the narcissist's life, "Stop" signs are meant for everyone else.

Because narcissist's have no ability to self-regulate their own behaviors, you sometimes have to set the parameters for them.

Narcissists proceed through some signals in life with the style and grace of a bulldozer. If they see or sense a "Stop" sign, they run it over and keep going.

Rather than running interference on all of these behaviors, sometimes you give a little leeway to the narcissist. I call it the "Here...but no farther..." approach.

You may let the narcissist have her way on a holiday or a vacation. Or perhaps you let him handle some issue with the children at school. Whatever the event may be, you give the narcissist a little space in which to operate. This is important for your own time and resources. Otherwise, you run the risk of constantly battling and controlling the narcissist.

You let the narcissist have some slack; however, you know where the rope ends. In your mind, you are clear about what is "far enough" and what is "too far".

For example, if the narcissist insists where everyone should go for a holiday, and you want to go, then let the narcissist decide. But, the narcissist does NOT get to set the agenda for everyone each and every day of the holiday. "Here...but no farther..."

You quit some battles in order to win your time, space, and life back.

I set the appropriate parameters of my life.

Well, It Ought to Be True!

What is the truth? Whatever the narcissist wants it to be.

Narcissists are like young children. When they want something to be true, they simply, in their mind, think it is true.

Narcissists do not look at how things actually are. Narcissists go through life interacting with things as they "ought to be" according to the narcissist.

If the narcissist wants to believe his or her child is gifted academically, and the child performs average in school, the narcissist does not see the true academic performance. The narcissist continues to act as if the child were brilliant because that is how it "ought to be".

If the narcissist is expected to pay a certain level of taxes, he or she will not. The taxes the narcissist does pay are in proportion to what the tax rate "ought to be", according to the narcissist.

If a narcissist does not want to follow an established rule, he or she will not. The rule is in the way of how things "ought to be".

If the narcissist does not like parts of your personality, you need to get rid of those parts, so your actions and behaviors can be as they "ought to be", according to the narcissist.

Laws, rules, and the truth mean nothing to a narcissist when compared to the narcissist's internal guiding compass of how things "ought to be".

I do not follow the distorted "truths" of others.

Nonstick-coating

In the narcissist's mind, what is the perfect gift? A scapegoat.

If there is anything a narcissist loves, it's a good scapegoat.

What could be better for a narcissist than to find someone to blame for all the problems, shortcomings, annoyances and inconveniences in the narcissist's life?

Anyone will do, even their own children. You can't have Mommy or Daddy looking bad when a completely defenseless person is in the home who can serve to take the blame for everyone.

Most likely, you have served as the scapegoat a time or two (or more) for the narcissist in your life.

Don't let this continue happening to you.

The narcissist may throw blame your way, but you can refuse to get stuck with it. You no longer defend, excuse, or explain yourself in order for the narcissist to stop blaming you. You simply refuse to accept any projected or contrived blame from the narcissist.

You are to become the nonstick-coated scapegoat.

I am impervious to the attempted attacks to blame and shame by others.

Quicksand

So much of the narcissist's persona and way of being are trappings in the making.

Narcissists are very skilled at getting what they want.

They prefer you give it to them willingly. If this fails, the narcissist has no problem setting a trap that extracts what he or she needs. Narcissists create chaos and drama. Before you know it, your time and energy are swept towards the narcissistic vortex.

Too often, we act as a "first responder" for the narcissist.

We rush into the drama and trauma trying to do "damage control". In typical "fight and flight" mode, we think we MUST do something, because that is what the narcissist wants.

But, perhaps a better response is to first do nothing.

Don't participate in the conversation offering strategies and hope. Don't suggest ways you can help. Don't recommend solutions or, heaven forbid, begin to enact any solutions.

Narcissistic drama is quicksand. The more you try to move, the more you are going to be sucked under.

When you stop moving, you allow your sense of self and the situation to stabilize.

Before moving into a situation, I make certain I am on solid ground.

Death by a 1,000 Paper Cuts

Narcissists train you to expect pain and to believe it is normal.

Although at times overtly aggressive in their maneuverings, narcissists can also be maestros of subtlety. If the knockout blow isn't convenient at the moment for the narcissist, he or she opts for small, "innocent" digs, innuendos, snide and snarky comments.

These small cuts to your spirit are designed to wear you down. The narcissist will deny this, and seek to reassure you that you are "too sensitive" and that these attacks can't hurt "that much".

These symbolic paper cuts don't hurt "that much", because they are not designed to cause massive pain. The little cuts and digs by a narcissist are meant to serve as a warning. By causing "small" harm, the narcissist tells you, "I will hurt you and I decide how much and when."

For someone who has experienced abuse, a loss between stimulus-response conditioning occurs. You become trained to respond "normally" to completely abnormal stimuli and vice versa.

Thus, the "little" acts of harm by the narcissist begin to go unnoticed by you. In this way, you are trained to accept threat and pain inflicted by others. Neither of these have a place in your life- ever.

Don't be fooled by the "little" attacks of a narcissist. These attacks are symbolic paper airplanes thrown at your head to warn you, the next one may be a bomb.

I am aware of how the actions and words of others impact me.

Frozen

Narcissist lie ALL THE TIME. It's what they do.
You know this. Truly, you do.

The fact narcissists lie all the time is not the true burden, because we understand this is what narcissists do.

What tends to wear us down, though, is deciding what to do with the lies.

When a narcissist lies to you, your options are reduced to two. You can either validate the lie, that is, go along with the lie, or you can acknowledge the lie for what it is- a lie.

When you choose the second choice, you sign on for a major battle.

A narcissist's sense of survival is threatened when he or she is called out on a lie. A life and death struggle (symbolically) ensues within the psyche of the narcissist, which is then projected onto you.

So, you end up feeling frozen when the narcissist lies to you. Do you accept the lie and by doing so, lend your support to something that is not real?
Or do you challenge the lie and prepare for a major fight?

Neither choice is appealing, yet the narcissist asks you to keep making it. Unfreeze yourself by acknowledging what is happening to you, and then decide what is best for you.

No matter what anyone attempts to do to hide it, the truth exists.

Scorekeeping System

Narcissists are life's ultimate scorekeeper.

Narcissists love keeping score in life, down to the tiniest details. Of course, they keep score in such a way that they always win.

The problems begin when we believe in the narcissist's scoring system.

Narcissists often introduce their scoring system into the relationship early on- a testing of the waters, if you will. They ask you to pay your share on some ridiculously small item. Or they present one small task they did for you as a testament to how much you "owe" them. Over time, the scorekeeping escalates until you are symbolically way behind.

By telling you that you are on the losing end of their convoluted scoring system, narcissists keep you hooked into doing and giving more, as you try to even the score.

You give. You give some more. And the deficit never lessens. The best approach is simple - exit the scoring system. Evaluate your behaviors on YOUR terms, not the narcissist's.

You do not "owe" anyone. Much to a narcissist's surprise, this sentiment also extends to him or her.

I arrived in the Universe as a free entity and that is how I shall remain.

Box of Paradox

Narcissists are a paradox of paradoxes.

Narcissism is a box of paradox. Behaviors and actions have multiple upon multiple conflicting meanings and messages.

The narcissist is at once overbearing, while also being completely absent. The narcissist is self-centered with no self-awareness. The narcissist's agendas are obvious and covert at the same time.

As we deal with the paradoxical nature of narcissism, we may begin to judge our own responses to the narcissist's confusing and inconsistent behaviors.

Perhaps you have been like me. At times, I have lied and hidden things from the narcissist in order to keep the peace. Other times, I have confronted, stormed out and threatened. I have also gone out of my way to please and help the narcissist.

I used to question this spectrum of behaviors. What was wrong with me that I could not select a certain approach with the narcissist and stick with it?

Given that narcissists exist within a paradoxical context, we can not expect our responses to them to always be linear and rationale. Within the box of paradox, we often have to choose from a rather random assortment of behavior options. Sometimes it can mean confrontation. At other times, it can mean placating the narcissist. Paradoxical behaviors require paradoxical responses.

I honor that in any given situation I am free to respond as needed based on my principles, understanding, and awareness.

Better think Once, Better think Twice

If necessity is the mother of invention, preparation is the father for handling a narcissist.

Whenever I receive an e-mail or phone call from a narcissist, I have in mind a follow-up question I silently ask myself "What is the back story here?"

Narcissists are masters at misdirection and deception. If you interact with a narcissist long enough, you know that the surface veneer does not reflect the depth of chaos underneath. For our own sanity, we must lift up that superficial cover to see what lies beneath.

If the narcissist calls and suddenly seems kind, gracious, and willing to help out, it is our job to stop, think once about what the narcissist's true motives may be (before getting excited the narcissist may be changing!), and then think twice about how we want to respond.

By slowing down to ask ourselves what really may be going on, we take the narcissist's power of surprise and "blink and you miss it approach" to a deceptive life.

One of the worst things is when we are duped by a narcissist and then transform this into self-criticism such as, "Why didn't I see that coming?" Use your powers of experience and awareness to help you understand the narcissist's motive and what he or she may be planning next.

When we engage our powers of thought, experience, and awareness, we are less likely to be victimized.

My prior experiences can be used to help me understand the current situation.

Dramatic License

Narcissists follow scripted procedures for creating drama.

Watch any movie or read a book designed to produce drama and you find the dramatic arc centers on one or both of the following: information that is misleading or missing and time is limited.

Why are these points common in dramatic features? They work. If it works for movies and books, it certainly works for the narcissist in your life.

Narcissists are pros at misleading or missing information. They say one thing and mean another. They "forget" to tell you something. They "accidentally" leave out important details.

If that does not create enough drama, the narcissist throws in the crunch of time. Narcissists delay and delay and then scream at everyone, "You are making me late." The narcissist may also demand a decision on an important matter (one with misleading or missing information) immediately. You are chastised for being "slow" if you want some time to decide.

Don't be bullied by these drama tactics and do not be caught up in the drama contrived by these tactics.

Take the time you need and find the information you need in order to make any and all decisions. The type of drama created by misinformation or limited times serves books and movies well. These do not, however, need to serve as the central plot of your life.

I deserve complete, accurate information and time before I make any decisions.

Wanting the Cake and Eating it, Too

Narcissists attempt to control everything, including your responses.

Narcissists, as you know, attempt to control everything in their environment, and this, of course, includes your behaviors. Often overlooked is a very specific aspect of your behavior that the narcissist desperately wants to control.

Narcissists want complete control over your responses to their behavior.

Narcissists give themselves permission to act in any way they desire- no matter how inappropriate or hurtful. You, however, are not given the permission to choose how to respond to the narcissist's behavior.

Basically, narcissists want their behavioral cake and to eat it, too.

None of us get this free pass in life. Yes, we are all free to choose our behaviors. What is not free for us to choose is the response of others to our behaviors. When we act obnoxiously, we are treated as if we are obnoxious. When we lie, people respond to us as if we tell lies.

Narcissists struggle to grasp this concept. Being unable to control the responses of others to their extreme behaviors is a serious trigger for most narcissists. They can not handle their behaviors being judged unfavorably or met with criticism. They insist that everyone understand and support their behaviors. When this does not happen, narcissistic rage is stirred.

In this, like most things the narcissist is confused. Narcissists, like all of us, have complete control. But, that control only extends to our own behaviors.

My responses to another's behaviors are my choice and my choice alone to make.

When the Going gets Crazy…Leave

You can not heal in the presence of someone who is unsafe to you.

Undertaking your healing journey in the presence of someone who is harmful to you is not healthy.

This statement seems to be obvious, but it was years before I embraced this idea.

For some reason, I thought it would be quitting if I removed myself from harm in order to heal. I worried more about the well-being of the other person than I did my own. I also wanted to prove to myself that I was better than any trauma inflicted upon me.

In some ways, I believe I saw healing in the face of such direct harm to be a mark of success. I had created a loop that said "If I can heal here, I can heal anywhere."

I now realize how distorted such thinking was.

Healing is about you and only you.

When you make healing a priority, you understand that placing yourself in the best possible environment is tantamount to your success. You deserve people in your life who support your healing, not undermine it.

My healing becomes easier and more effective when I am in a safe environment with supportive people.

Survival Shell

We give up a lot of things, in the mistaken belief that we must do so in order to ensure our survival.

Living or interacting with a narcissist requires certain skills.

Unfortunately, one skill that may develop is the giving up of one's self in an attempt to ensure one's survival.

Have you given up joy in life, because you believe you need to be on guard and living in fear in order to survive?

Have you given up taking care of yourself, so you can do for others, in the hopes of continuing your survival?

Have you given up bits and pieces of yourself along the way so others would "tolerate" you better and thus, again, be assured in some way of your survival?

Have you given up your own needs, so you can be indispensable to others, increasing the odds of your survival?

I wonder what you have given up in order to "survive".

As we learn and grow, we come to the awareness that our TRUE survival depends on retrieving those parts of ourselves that we once gave up.

All parts of my Being are essential to my sense of wholeness. I need not give up pieces of myself for others.

Why "No Contact" requires Your Effort

The "no contact" agreement is not between you and the narcissist; it is between you and only you.

Often, once we get a handle on narcissism, we decide to institute "no contact" (or as limited contact as possible) with the narcissist.

At this point, our intentions are clear. We do not open ourselves to phone calls, phone messages, texts, conversations, pleas, threats and arguments. If because of life dynamics, we still interact with the narcissist, we keep such engagements well-defined.

And then, often, the narcissist gets quiet, and so does our resolve.

We are driven by a need to relate, and we hate to exclude anyone (even at risk to our well- being). So we begin to think it may not be as bad as we remember. We open ourselves to a little engagement with the narcissist, and the problems begin.

After you initiate no or little contact, you can not go back.

If you engage in contact (beyond your set limitations) even once, be prepared to re-establish your boundaries several times over. You may, in your mind, think you are initiating contact "just this one time". This means absolutely nothing to the narcissist. Narcissism is a many-headed monster that demands to be fed. If you throw out a scrap or two, the narcissist comes looking for more.

The decision of "no contact' is for YOUR benefit, not the narcissist's. You made an agreement with yourself. Honor it.

I honor the decisions I make and do not confuse myself by negating these decisions.

Trust in the Un-trustable

Dealing with a narcissist involves handling the predictably unpredictable.

Narcissists do not follow typical relational patterns, thus we can not relax, trusting in the relationship skills we have developed over a lifetime.

Although narcissists do not respond in a "typical" fashion, they, like everyone else, fall into patterned behaviors. It's just that, unlike most, the patterned behaviors are destructive and self-centered.

A therapist I know once said, "Trust in someone does necessarily mean the person is *trustworthy*. Trust is when you have faith that the person will act and behave in a consistent pattern."

Narcissists are not trust*worthy*. They lie, they hide, they blame. However, because they so consistently use these behaviors, we can begin to trust the narcissist to act in a predictable manner. By trusting the narcissist to act as expected, we move from shock and surprise to proactive preparation.

Otherwise, too often, we are caught off- guard thinking, "I can't believe they did that!" Of course the narcissist did "that". Whatever the "that" is, the narcissist has likely engaged in the behavior before.

When we trust the narcissist to act as expected, we move to awareness and on to planning. We know what may happen, so we must ask ourselves "How would I like to prepare?"

I am not surprised and caught off-guard when others behave as expected.

There Goes the Vesica Pisces

*Narcissists operate under the belief of
"What is mine is mine and what is yours is mine, also."*

When two circles partially overlap, the portion in the center is called a *vesica pisces*. Symbolically, the vesica pisces represents the balance between union and separation.

In a relationship with a narcissist, this balance becomes highly distorted as the narcissist eclipses your life. The vesica pisces is all but obliterated, as the narcissist's circle consumes yours.

A healthy union between two whole and complete individuals, honoring a separate space for each, is a foreign idea to a narcissist.

A narcissist sees no one or no thing existing outside of him or herself. Thus, the narcissist sees no issue with taking over your life. They are claiming what is theirs in the first place.

You can not allow your life to be eclipsed by the narcissist's need to "own" you.

If the narcissist is to remain in your life, keep the symbol of the vesica pisces in mind. A space can exist for your lives to overlap, but you have a part of you which always remains separate.

I engage with relationships in a way that balances union and separation.

Center Management

Narcissists always require management. ALWAYS.

When you are in a relationship with a narcissist, you can not allow the narcissist to manage the area where your lives intersect and overlap.

The narcissist can not handle managing relationships. Narcissists have no ability to effectively manage themselves, let alone effectively manage engagements with others.

Narcissists control, belittle, demean, demand and so on, but they can not truly relate. Thus, you can not leave your relationship under the narcissist's direction and control.

We would all enjoy living in the idealistic world of light and love, even when dealing with a narcissist. Idealism is not realism, though. You can live in your idealistic world on your own, but when your world overlaps with a narcissist, it is YOUR responsibility to become realistic.

You can not hand over the relationship reins to the narcissist, while you stand by. In the area of relationships, narcissists always require management. They simply do not have the skill set required for success.

When you give up your responsibility for relationship management to the narcissist, you give up your power as well.

I believe in my ability to manage relationships. I step forward to handle situations that affect my well-being.

Deal with the Devil

The contractual agreement with a narcissist goes something like this-
Agree with me or you are dead to me.

Having a relationship with a narcissist is making a deal with the devil.
You reject yourself so the narcissist will have you.

We acquiesce to the narcissist's wishes in big and small ways because the
narcissist presents with the ultimate threat- the removal of love. The
proverbial sword hanging over everyone's head is the awareness that the
narcissist will reject and disown a person who does not comply with
narcissist's wishes.

Some are strong enough to walk away from this swaying sword. Others are
not.

So, the deal is made. You agree to give up huge parts of yourself, so the
narcissist keeps you. At its core, narcissism is an existential crisis. The
narcissist is forever and always in a life-threatening survival mode (in their
minds). So they take- ruthlessly and fearfully- because if you don't give,
they cease to exist (in their minds).

If upon interacting with a narcissist, you felt as if you lost pieces of
yourself, you most likely did. It was the price you were expected to pay
for the "deal" made.

I am free to exit agreements that no longer serve my higher purpose.

The Dollhouse Effect

Narcissists treat people like dolls, one-dimensional objects, with a role and place assigned by the narcissist.

When a child plays with a doll, the doll has no role other than the one created by the child. The doll can be a baby, a friend, a student, and so on. The doll can be "good" one day and "very bad" the next.

Whatever the child's imagination thinks, the doll becomes. The doll, of course, has no say, and thus beautifully exemplifies how narcissists treat us.

We are one-dimensional objects in the narcissist's dollhouse world. The narcissist believes he or she can project any number of roles upon us and we will fulfill them. Our consent is never sought nor considered.

The narcissist also attempts to control our image in the world, and whether we are to be seen as "very good" or "very bad". And like the dolls with which a child plays, the narcissist believes he or she has complete control over where we are placed. The narcissist regulates our comings and goings and who we are allowed to see.

A child learns, though, that there is a whole world beyond the dollhouse of the child's imagination. The delight in life comes from interacting with this world. But narcissists never grow out of childhood and prefer to remain in their dollhouse world.

Narcissists never understand we were only doll-like in their minds, never our own.

The roles I play in life are of my own choosing and creation.

The Disconnect Effect

Narcissists love to take things apart, including your sense of self.

Gaping wounds develop when we interact with a narcissist, as the narcissist attempts to disconnect parts of ourselves. The following disconnections are commonly observed:

The narcissist attempts to disconnect you from your own awareness. You may think you saw or experienced something, the narcissist insists otherwise. The narcissist tells you that your experiences and perceptions are somehow "wrong" and "not real".

The narcissist attempts to disconnect your actions from your intentions. You may begin an endeavor with the most sincere of intentions. The narcissist distorts and manipulates even the best of intentions into something dark and crazy.

The narcissist attempts to disconnect your words from their meaning. You may be eloquent, you may be articulate, and all your words bang and clang around in the narcissist's mind as he or she comes up with his or her own interpretation.

The narcissist attempts to disconnect behaviors from context. If you behave in a certain way because of the context, the narcissist shows your actions to be wrong. Narcissists make up their own rules and criticize you if you don't play along.

The narcissist attempts to disconnect your emotions from your heart. Where you once saw yourself as loving and compassionate, spending time with a narcissist has you doubting these things about yourself. Every one of your emotions is open to narcissistic criticism and correction.

I am whole and intact. My awareness, actions, words, behaviors and emotions function in wholeness.

Plug and Play Method of Narcissists

A narcissist views relationships as plug and play devices.

When you are in a relationship with a narcissist, both you and the relationship are viewed as "things" by the narcissist.

Narcissists relate to objects, not people.

Thus, in the narcissist's life, people and relationships are similar to electronic "plug and play" devices.

As a plug and play device, your sole purpose is to perform for the narcissist without any real input, upkeep, or engagement from the narcissist.

The narcissist "plugs" you in, and you are expected to "play" without problems. If you cause too much hassle for the narcissist, you are "unplugged" and forgotten, similar to the failed electronics littering some households.

Ever wonder how a narcissist moves on so quickly after a relationship ends? Simple. They find a new device to plug in.

And that new device, I guarantee you, performs the exact some function as you did in the narcissist's life. The narcissist never changes, they simply move on and find different devices with which to play.

I create relationships of depth and meaning. I am too important to be someone's "plug and play" device.

Interior Decorating

Narcissists are the interior decorators of the psyche, always moving around the mirrors for better reflection.

Narcissists love to look into the mirrors they have created. The mirrors include anyone in the narcissist's sphere of control.

Narcissists, like an interior decorator of the mind and psyche, place these mirrors where they think the mirrors give the best reflection. This may mean dressing up their children to "play a part", insisting a spouse look and act a "certain way", and demanding almost parrot-like responses to their demands.

When the mirrors fail to do their part (i.e. reflect back to the narcissist as the narcissist desires), the mirrors are deemed "broken", and more often than not, "beyond repair".

The mirror may in fact be deadly accurate in its reflection of the narcissist, but in the narcissist's world, accurate reflection has no role in the purpose of a mirror. The mirror is to reflect only what the narcissist desires.

You have a strong mind that reflects upon what you witness. Place yourself in the position to give the most accurate reflection, not the reflection the narcissist desires.

To the best of my ability, I witness with accuracy.

Echo…Echo…Echo..

Narcissists do not hear the original words, they only hear the echo.

The character of Echo is relevant to the story of Narcissus for a number of reasons. Beyond the mythological character of Echo, we can also look at the physical nature of echoes and how these apply to living with a narcissist.

Once, I heard a young child yell, "Echo…Echo…" in an empty staircase. His "echo-s" were of course met with resounding "echo-s" reverberating through the space.

As I tried to call to this child, I realized I could not be heard over the "echo-s", and I realized this exemplifies talking to a narcissist. Your words are not heard. Reverberating through the narcissist's head are the echoes of ideas about how the world should be, how the world has failed them, how misunderstood they are, how everyone else has problems that in turn are causing THEM problems, and so on, and so on, and so on.... echo...echo...echo...

If you are like me, you have perhaps tried different tactics to gain the narcissist's attention. It's like banging a cymbal in an echo chamber. No matter what technique you use, nothing is heard.

My concern is that the narcissist's lack of attention to our words can be transmuted into a sense that we are not communicating clearly or are not worth listening to. Neither of these things is true.

The problem is not you and your communication skills, the problem lies within the echo chamber of the narcissist's mind.

I speak my ideas with authenticity and sincerity. Someone's lack of attention is not a reflection of my value and worth.

Severing Instincts

To relate to a narcissist, you must cut away at your relational instincts.

Whether you are consciously aware of it or not, you operate under a certain set of expectations of how others relate and respond to you and vice versa.

Relationships require a give and take that we have, for the most part, been learning throughout our lives. Years and years of training have taken place, which may be to your detriment when dealing with a narcissist. Many of the relationships skill you have worked to hone, such as communication, compromise, and resolution, fall flat with a narcissist.

When attempting to manage a relationship with a narcissist, you must begin to understand that your normal relational skills will not bring you expected results. Where you seek compromise, the narcissist seeks total victory. Where you seek understanding, the narcissist seeks domination.

This can be a difficult realization to make and a difficult habit to break as our social interactions and expectations are so ingrained.

Freedom from narcissistic manipulation often requires us to sever our instinctual relationship responses. We must cut away at how we believe relationships "should be" and so we can effectively relate to what is before us.

I am capable of using different skills to manage different relationships.

Parting is Such Sweet Awesomeness

Narcissists never believe you will leave- until you do.

For all of its challenges, leaving a relationship with a narcissist can be difficult.   You most likely at one point loved this individual. Now, you know the pain and harm such people cause.

Once you make the decision to leave a narcissist, you may find your exit catches the narcissist by surprise. Narcissists are not good losers, and when they have lost someone as special as you, they are especially sore.

A primary control mechanism of every narcissist is fear and threats; so of course, you can expect to suffer these if you leave. This is when you must realize the best defense is a good offense.

Be proactive. You, more than anyone, know and understand the capabilities of the narcissist. Do not fool yourself, prepare yourself.

Think about where you are vulnerable and formulate a strategy to protect those areas. Lean on friends and loved ones as you need. Take the guess work out of momentary decisions by having a plan and sticking to it. Create reminders to fortify yourself when you think about wavering and returning to this relationship.

At the end of the day, "Parting is such sweet awesomeness" because regardless of the status of the narcissist, you part ways with your old self, the one who was confused by narcissism and did not understand the power you had.

The internal changes I make lead to outward changes, as well.

Follow the "Leader"

Narcissists love to lead and boldly go where no one wants them.

As narcissists see everyone as part of themselves, being the "leader" comes quite naturally to narcissists. In the narcissist's mind, the narcissist is ALWAYS the leader, because no one else exists.

Narcissists have no introspection, little self-awareness, and even less concern for others. None of this deters them from seeing themselves as good leaders. The only time narcissists don't like to lead is when there are problems. Issues that tarnish the narcissist's grandiose self-image are particularly problematic for the narcissist.

When problems arise, the narcissistic leader hides.

Narcissists are not captains that go down with their ship. No, they are the captain already in the lifeboat, blaming everyone in their wake. You can not trust narcissists to lead you, so don't let them.

Leadership requires awareness and concern for others. Neither of these are strong suits of the narcissist.

If you need to, humor the narcissist into believing he or she is the leader. Then, take command of the ship yourself, before the narcissist runs it aground.

I am the captain of my lie. I do not need to take directions or leadership from harmful people.

Knife Play

A narcissist's approach is to not remove the wounding knife, but rather to twist it.

Narcissists are sadistic. Do not lie to yourself about this, and do not allow others to tell you otherwise for convenience.

If you witness narcissists, and remove all excuses and explanations for their behaviors, you conclude that narcissists take pleasure in causing pain to others.

We all wound one another inadvertently. It is part of being human. However most of us, upon realizing we hurt another, seek to make amends.

Not narcissists. They see the knife wound, and rather than applying compression, they twist the blade. Of course, often, narcissists try to keep this sadistic side of themselves hidden.

If you look closely enough, though, you see the narcissist inflicting pain, but never once seeking to lessen it. (This is completely counter, of course, to the five-alarm response the narcissist expects when he or she is wounded).

Someone, who not only willing causes you pain, but also *takes pleasure* in this pain is not someone you need in your life.

I remove harmful people from my life.

Word Alert

The narcissist has often commandeered the vocabulary in order to control the situation.

For those who experience narcissistic abuse, it is difficult to find the vocabulary to express the terror and horror one experiences. On the surface, things may look acceptable. Certainly the narcissist has a hand in this perception by others. You must remember that to the narcissist, how he or she is *perceived* is more important than how he or she really *is*.

Narcissists often speak the "right" words as a set-up for their culminating destructive act. Victims of narcissism know this.

In fact, most victims have in their minds a type of threat assessment scale devoted to the narcissist's words and tone of voice. Certain words are a clear signal that the safety of "green" has transitioned to "yellow". When the words and tone escalate just enough, the victim knows that "red", full-blown narcissistic rage, is not far behind.

Those unfamiliar with narcissism think the words and phrases of the narcissist are innocuous. Those who interact with narcissists know different. They have learned to read the terrifying messages between the lines and lips of the narcissist.

Narcissists have coded talk and use very, very specific words known to impact the victim.

I am not confused or frightened by the "hidden" messages others send me.

Flying Solo

Narcissists seldom fly solo; they recruit others into their flight plan.

Narcissists are often discussed in relation to their "flying monkeys". Flying monkeys are people recruited by the narcissist to do the narcissist's bidding.

Flying monkeys tell lies for the narcissist, seek to protect the narcissist, and initiate and maintain smear campaigns against anyone who disagrees with the narcissist. The only agenda of the flying monkey is to keep the narcissist happy. Not that this action is altruistic. By keeping the narcissist happy, the flying monkeys believe they are assured spots in the "special" circle of those favored by the narcissist.

Flying monkeys use the fantasy purported by the narcissist to feel "liked". It is a feather in the flying monkey's cap to have remained in favor of the narcissist. The flying monkey can then look down upon all the others who have not fared as well.

If you are not part of the flying monkey corps, the flying monkeys work to convince you of how great the narcissist is and how wrong you are. Your agreement with them ensures your inclusion in the flight plan. If you refuse to play along with the idea that the narcissist is perfect, the flying monkeys reject you and fly bombing runs upon your character and psyche.

Because flying monkeys are so aligned with the narcissist, you can not allow them substantial space in your life. Whenever possible ignore these types.

Handling the narcissist is enough. You do not need additional flight interference to your trajectory.

I can fly solo in life and I can also choose who flies with me.

Flying Blind

Narcissists insist that those who follow them remain blind to them.

The narcissist uses the eyes of others in order to be seen in a certain way. Otherwise, the narcissist insists you remain blind.

As part of the narcissist's inner circle, "flying monkeys" are blind to the narcissist. Flying monkeys are people who see the narcissist as the narcissist *desires* to be seen.

Just as the narcissist can not truly see his or her own reflection, these flying monkeys are flying blind through life. They have to be blind to the narcissist's true self if they are to maintain their position.

As we begin to heal on our own journeys, we can take it upon ourselves to enlighten others. In other words, where the flying monkey is blind, we attempt to help them see.

We may dislike seeing others still being supportive of the narcissist. We may sense others are unaware of who the narcissist is and want to warn them. In addition, as we remove ourselves from the narcissist's sphere, we long to help others escape, so as to avoid the pain and confusion we know is coming.

But, as we let go of the narcissist in our lives, we also must let go of trying to rescue any flying monkeys. Flying monkeys have made the decision to fly blind, and we are not the ones to remove the covering of their eyes.

I honor that each person can form their own impressions of others. I am not obligated in any manner to alter these perceptions.

Peter Pan Syndrome

Narcissists never grow up.

Although narcissists appear as functioning adults on the surface, underneath they function at a much lower development level. In some ways, narcissists remind me of teenagers. They display moments of clarity and maturity, but for the most part, adult development remains years away.

When you become frustrated with how the narcissist is acting or responding, remind yourself that you are dealing with someone with a teenager's mentality. Before you allow the narcissist to handle an important task, ask yourself, "Would I allow a 12- year-old to complete this job?" If the answer is "No", then don't (if at all possible) give the task to the narcissist.

You are not making excuses for the narcissist, nor are you pitying the narcissist and letting him or her off the hook. What you are doing is building a reasonable, truthful context.

If you continue to act and treat the narcissist as if he or she has adult skills, you end up suffering in the end, not the narcissist. Narcissists are too self-centered to allow themselves to suffer for long. You, on the other hand, are left picking up the symbolic teenager's mess.

Your clarity about the narcissist and his or her behaviors does not solve the problem of these behaviors. However, your clarity enables engagement with a narcissist that meets the narcissist on his or her level.

I honor that we are each at different stages in our lives, and I create my responses accordingly.

Rudder-ed

Narcissists jam our "relational rudders" into a stuck position, throwing our navigation off.

Have you ever wondered why having a narcissist in your life takes up so much time? You see other relationships and think, "That seems so easy." You may even begin to question "What is wrong with me that I would even need a book of mantras for dealing with a narcissist?"

Well, the problem is not you. The problem is that if you interact with a narcissist long enough, your "relational rudder" gets locked into the wrong position.

Our "relational rudder" helps us sail through the social and emotional interactions of our lives. We have been learning to use this rudder since we were children. When we interact with narcissists, though, we constantly must correct our relational course.

Narcissists are relational rogue waves, striking us broadside, knocking us off track. When we adapt to narcissistic behaviors for consistent and prolonged periods, our relational rudder can become stuck in a compromising position.

We travel circles trying to find our bearings emotionally. We begin to question and second guess "normal" responses. In time, the adjustment required to counteract a narcissist drains our energy.

As we disengage from narcissistic interactions, part of our growth and recovery involves reorienting our misaligned relational rudder to direct us towards fulfilling and positive relationships.

I navigate my relationships with dignity and grace.

Love and Value…Love and Value

A narcissist is someone who cares enough to do the very least.

"Love"

There may be no other word that keeps up hooked into narcissistic relationships more than this single word.

Narcissists use the word "love" to explain away their poor behaviors and to make us feel as if we must continue to commit to and support the narcissists. After all, they "love" us.

We experience a tremendous amount of disconnect between the spoken word of "love" and the narcissist's actions. We fill in the gaps with explanations, or we try even harder to win the narcissist's "love".

The "love" that a narcissist professes becomes an issue of semantics. Sometimes it helps to substitute another word for this "love". The word I choose is "value". The narcissist may "love" you, but does the narcissist "value" you?

To a narcissist, love and value, love and value, go together like oil and water. The narcissist values no one but himself or herself.

Exchanging the word "value" for "love" enables you to gain clarity into how exactly the narcissist is treating you.

Can anyone truly love you, if they do not value you?

I honor the meaning that the word "love" holds for me.

Mirror, Broken

Narcissists love mirrors, not self-reflection.

The mirror of self-reflection exists in our own minds. The narcissist's mirror, though, becomes damaged during development, thus, making accurate self-reflection impossible. Because the narcissist is incapable of honest self-reflection, the narcissist is stuck.

To grow, one needs a sense of awareness beyond the current state of "self". The space "beyond self" is a foreign land that does not exist to the narcissist.

Compounding this problem is the fact that the narcissist has no ability to integrate feedback from the outside. Anytime a person attempts to give critical feedback, the narcissist can not integrate it. The incoming signals are simply lost or destroyed.

If narcissists can not self-reflect and can not take feedback from others, how exactly are narcissists to grow? They can't.

Therefore, you can not expect the narcissist to grow and change. Remove your energy from such expectations and place that energy where it belongs- on you and your growth.

I am not responsible for the ability of others to grow. My time and energy go towards my own growth.

Preemptive Strike

Narcissists are the illusionist upon the cosmic stage.

Narcissists manipulate and create fantasy worlds. However, even narcissists have limits. When the fantasy world of a narcissist is in jeopardy and despite their BEST efforts, everything is unraveling and the truth is going to emerge- the narcissist will NOT fess up.

Instead, the narcissist issues a preemptive strike.

Normally, the narcissist keeps everything hidden. But when he or she is backed into a corner, the narcissist attempts to get your thinking, emotions, and heart headed in the opposite direction of the real issue.

The preemptive strike is a trick used by narcissists everywhere to divert your time, energy and focus from the issue at hand. You experience a preemptive strike when the narcissist brings up a topic seemingly out of nowhere with great urgency. After you disengage from the narcissist, your first thought is "Huh...I wonder what that was all about?"

The preemptive strike- accusing you of something random, ranting and raving at some weird concern- is the symbolic wand waving of a narcissist in illusionist mode. As your head, symbolically and literally, turns towards this distraction and drama, the narcissist uses the momentum to pull you away from paying attention to the truth.

The preemptive strike is a warning that something is going to be revealed. Use this common narcissistic trick to your advantage. When you sense a preemptive strike, don't distract yourself, prepare yourself.

I use my intellect, instincts, and awareness to observe what is happening before me.

The Elephant in the Room

The narcissist's personality IS the problem.

Narcissism isn't an insignificant personality glitch, like having the uncle who drinks a bit too much at social gatherings or the cousin who can't seem to stop telling off-color jokes.

Narcissism isn't some slight issue you can work around, because narcissism encompasses EVERYTHING.

Narcissism is the proverbial elephant in the room. No one wants to mention it, but it takes up a great deal of space and crowds everything else out.

Trying to relate to the narcissist by maneuvering around the narcissism is like navigating around an elephant in the living room. With a great sense of hope, you push the elephant to the side of the room, only to realize with an elephant, there is no "side" of the room. Elephant tissue fills every space.

The same occurs with narcissism. Narcissism is not limited to a little "side" of someone's life. It is their life.

As with the elephant in the room, removing all the furniture does not help either. No matter how many things you take out of your life, there is never enough space for the narcissist.

My life is open and expansive, with space for those who matter to me.

Propaganda

Narcissists do not use truth. Narcissists do not use facts. Narcissists use propaganda.

Many of us enter conversations and interactions looking for common ground. Narcissists do not look for common ground, they look to ground you down until you acquiesce and say they are "right".

Narcissists do not worry about truth or facts. Narcissists worry about their agenda.

To further their agenda, narcissists pulverize you with propaganda. Like a plane overhead dropping leaflets, narcissists bombard you with their point of view. It does not matter to the narcissist if the message is right. The only thing that matters is that you believe the message.

This propaganda-making of narcissists also explains why they change course and reverse their message at a moment's notice. Consistency of the message is not part of the agenda for narcissists too busy metaphorically printing off propaganda pages.

No wonder the narcissist has likely accused you of never understanding what he or she is saying.

You have never understood, because it is all made up lies dropped into your life. You have known for a very long time that when a narcissist speaks, it is propaganda in the making.

I am immune to the propaganda of others.

Coup-countrecoup

Psychological coup-countrecoup occurs when the narcissist completely reverses direction.

Coup-countrecoup occurs in some forms of traumatic head injuries. Coup-countrecoup happens when the brain first strikes one side of the skull, only to rebound from the impact and strike the opposite side.

The back and forth striking of the brain within the skull cavity is an excellent analogy for the psychological injuries narcissists induce.

Narcissists expect us to engage fully in their lives. However, often, as soon as you lean in to commit- emotionally, financially, and mentally- to the narcissist's current plan, the narcissist reverses course and heads in the opposite direction. The person they at one time praised, now becomes someone they despise. The project they were once so excited about, no longer holds their attention, and so on.

Obviously, this change in direction is not conveyed to you. You flail in the wind, over-committing to the narcissist's original plan; only to be criticized by the narcissists for not understanding and embracing the new plan.

Back and forth, back and forth your psyche and energy go, developing coup-countrecoup injuries as you rebound from one plan to another. Committing time and energy to these endeavors only to witness a massive redirection is exhausting. Whenever you are party to the narcissist's initial interests, move with caution. Maintaining your center is the most effective way to lessen any psychological coup-contrecoup injuries.

I use a sense of caution before committing time and energy towards the endeavors of others.

PR Manager

Narcissists expect everyone to serve as their personal public relations mangers.

Interacting with a narcissist, requires you to fulfill (dare I say, "embrace") any number of roles dedicated to the narcissist's well-being.

One role you may overlook (but the narcissist has not) is the role of public relations manager for the narcissist.

Narcissists project the responsibility for *their* image upon everyone else.

No matter what behavior narcissists enact, they expect others to do more than simply accept the behaviors. They expect others to explain the behavior in such a way that the narcissist is seen in a positive light.

To the narcissist, the narcissist's behaviors are NEVER the issue. Your ability to manage the perception of the behaviors is the issue, as you are supposed to "spin it", so the narcissist looks good.

In the narcissist's mind, he or she has never done anything to warrant a negative reaction by any one. If a negative response ensues, the fault is yours for failing as the PR manager.

You, of course, are not responsible for the narcissist's image. Being the PR manager for the narcissist is a role from which you should gladly resign.

I take no responsibility for how others are perceived.

Standing

You always know where you stand with a narcissist- you are either the ally of the moment or the enemy of all eternity.

Our self-perception takes a hit when we relate with a narcissist. In normal everyday engagement, we use others to help build and mold our perceptions in a realistic manner.

We must remember, though, that a narcissist is not grounded in reality. Narcissists are grounded in their own self-centered, internal world. Therefore, whether the narcissist supports us or denigrates us, the acts and words have very little to do with who we are.

Every interaction with a narcissist centers on the narcissist and this includes when a narcissist talks to or about you. Until we realize this, we waste time and energy trying to convince the narcissist of who we truly are.

The narcissist's perception of you comes from within him or herself. It has nothing to do with you.

I am responsible for how I perceive myself.

Schrodinger's Cat

To a narcissist, "reality" only exists because the narcissist observed it.

You may be familiar with an experiment commonly referred to as "Schrodinger's Cat". In this thought experiment, an imaginary cat is sealed in a box containing poison and radioactivity. The cat either lives or dies. Given this experimental design, though, the determination of the cat's state is made by opening the box and observing the cat. Thus, the "observer effect" occurs.

Whenever I interact with narcissists, I think of Schrodinger's cat.

Narcissists create a particular perceived reality based on their own observations. Narcissists believe the observers (which would be them) determine reality.

The narcissist's observations need not be realistic or consistent. One moment, the narcissist declares the symbolic cat dead. So, you symbolically bury the "dead" cat. Next, the narcissist decides the symbolic cat is alive. You are now asked, symbolically, to unbury the "dead" (now "alive") cat.

What is important to remember is that the true state of the cat does not matter to the narcissist. The important point, to the narcissist, is that his or her observation *determines* reality. What also matters is that you believe and commit to narcissist's observations, otherwise known as "reality" to the narcissist.

I examine all evidence myself before concluding the state of matters in my life.

Why Narcissists need to be "Special"

Narcissists must always be considered "special" for one simple reason- they suck at being "normal".

I realize our definitions of "normal" vary. However, when you look at narcissists and how they try to interact with the world, you understand they deviate from the consensus of "normal". Their behaviors, emotions, and responses do not align with most people, who are maturing and evolving.

I wonder sometimes, if after failing so abysmally at the life and interactions we all enjoy, the narcissist, in some type of default mechanism, gives up.

As a defense mechanism, the narcissist declares "normal" as "wrong" and begins to self-define as "special". Basically, in a reverse of "If you can't beat them, join them", the narcissist decides, "If you can't join them, act superior to them."

In so many ways, narcissists can not join "normal". They simply do not have the skill set to do so. When I observe narcissists and see how they try to act normal, it is painfully obvious that it is all an act.

At some point, I think narcissists just give up trying to participate. They have no authentic way to engage with "normal", so they are left creating "special".

I welcome a sense of inclusiveness in my life. I realize "special" often breeds a sense of isolation.

Speaking the Language

Narcissists speak a language of fear and anger.

Within each of us, a part exists that believes we should always attempt goodness and kindness. We believe in rising above it all and taking the higher road. These, of course, are idealistic views. Something that pairs nicely with such idealism, though, is a dose of realism.

I know for myself, I have called forth some pretty base (and surprising to me) behaviors when dealing with a narcissist. Behaviors I believed I was "better than". I have threatened, screamed, and cursed (with a strength, conviction, and creativity I did not know I had). I have walked by and mentally (and physically, when I thought no one was looking) flipped them the bird. I have acted stone deaf and refused to make eye contact.

Why?

In some ways, I was "speaking" a language the narcissist understands. I was, whether I admitted it at the time, meeting the narcissist on the narcissist's level.

I used to sit and judge myself after these encounters. I wondered who I was that I acted "so mean" or said "those things".

But then I realized **there is no right or wrong when dealing with a narcissist. There is awareness and understanding that each moment may require a unique response from us.**

Some of these responses may include taking the higher ground. Some responses may be designed to be aggressive. The key, though, is that we do not further harm ourselves by judging our sincere efforts.

I honor the difficult choices required when interacting with a narcissist.
I free myself from harmful self-judgment.

Pre-Traumatic Stress Disorder

Narcissists love creating stress before the stressor.

We have all heard of PTSD (posttraumatic stress disorder). However, PTSD's cousin, Pre-TSD (pre-traumatic stress disorder), is still often overlooked. (In some ways, PTSD is the forefather of all Pre-TSD, but I think it is important to be aware of this specific aspect of stress.)

Pre-TSD, as the name implies, is the anticipatory rise in stress hormones and activation of the stress response prior to an event. Having a narcissist in your life places you in a constant state of Pre-TSD.

You are always waiting on high alert. Even when things are going "well", you know that "well" has an expiration date. So, you prepare yourself. You are in fight or flight mode days, weeks, months in advance.

The activation of the Pre-TSD response is unconscious. However, this does not mean this response is without cost. Living with anticipatory stress depletes us of our resources and our joy in life.

Bringing the Pre-TSD response into conscious awareness can help us mitigate the costs of this response. We can understand our stress response begins long before we are in direct contact with the narcissist. In this awareness, we can begin to formulate ways to lessen this stress. We can also honor the depletion of our resources that occurs with such stress and seek to fill ourselves in healthy ways.

The present moment is where I experience my power.

You say "Boundary", the Narcissist says "Violate"

A narcissist is more likely to see any boundaries you establish as "annoyances" rather than specific actions to protect your space.

To a narcissist, your separate space (and life) does not exist. A narcissist only sees things in relation to self, and all things, including people, are only relatable to the narcissist through their possible contribution to this sense of self.

Little tolerance exists within narcissists for things that are "theirs" (in their mind) that are not behaving as the narcissist desires. Your setting of a boundary is seen by the narcissist as a part of himself or herself "misbehaving".

A narcissist violates each and every one your boundaries in order to regain control- and this is important to note- of what they perceive as "theirs". If a narcissist happens to bang into one of your energetic boundaries, he or she will not take this as a sign to back off. In fact, your boundary incites the narcissist to even GREATER action to violate the boundary.

Over time, the repeated violation, or attempts to violate your boundaries, can make it seem as if the boundaries are useless. Never doubt your abilities to set boundaries. You and your boundaries are NOT the problem, the narcissist's self-perception is.

I set firm, consistent boundaries. Someone's lack of respect for these boundaries does not lessen the value of these boundaries.

The Boiling Frog Analogy in Reverse

The narcissist responds to any mishap with the intensity of a frog suddenly flung into boiling water.

If you place a frog in tepid water and slowly raise the temperature, the frog boils to death, never noting the small increases in temperature. Some equate living with a narcissist to this analogy. The stress and abuse do not begin at a boiling level; instead incremental increases occur along the way, until we are in symbolic boiling water.

For a narcissist under stress, the boiling frog analogy works in reverse.

A narcissist perceives even the slightest stressor (or symbolic rise in temperature) to be a substantial conflict. Even a life event that for most would fall under "lukewarm" has the narcissist flailing about as if his or her skin were scalding. No display of drama is too big or too demonstrative for a narcissist suffering a perceived stress.

We all have stressful times in life. Part of being a capable adult is realizing the world is not designed to simply accommodate our every whim.

Life challenges, both big and small, are to be expected. Our job is to grow and develop, so we handle the stresses and strains of life with compassion, understanding and awareness. Placed in the boiling cauldron of life, we work to survive in the most beautiful way we can.

The narcissist, having never grown up, continues to handle life stresses with drama. They flail about; sure they are boiling to death.

I choose to handle my life with grace and dignity, not stress and drama.

The Buffet

Narcissists are gluttons for the good parts of your life.

If the narcissist is to remain in your life, you need to decide how much access the narcissist has to your life.

Picture your life as a buffet.   Some people get to enjoy the entire buffet. Others, such as work colleagues, may be limited to appetizers, tidbits of your life, but not the main course.

Narcissists are gluttons, especially when it comes to the "good" things of others. They approach your life with an "all you can eat" mentality. However, it is your buffet and you decide who is served and what they are served.

If the narcissist must be in your life, you will not allow him to starve. However, you deny him access to all the best cuts of meat, delectable side dishes, and out of this world desserts that comprise your life.

Symbolically, give the narcissist the basics- a bit of chicken breast, a stalk or two of broccoli, and maybe, a slice of bread. Then, direct him away from any designs on the main courses of your life. Believe me, despite his protests, he will not starve.

Take things off the buffet table if you have to in order to keep your life free from narcissistic consumption. Not everyone deserves the desserts of your life.

I choose which pieces of my life and self I offer to others.

Throwing Good Energy after Bad

Throwing good energy in after the craziness...otherwise known as living with a narcissist.

We have all heard the saying about throwing good money after bad. Having a narcissist in your life has you enacting this process energetically. You throw good energy in after the narcissist's craziness.

After witnessing the narcissist's destructive acts, your first thought may be to use your good energy to clean up, clear up, prop up, dispose of, reform, cover up and/or conceal the mess made by the narcissist. We feel compelled to somehow "fix" all the narcissistic damage.

By bringing in our good energy, we believe we are showing the narcissist a different way of being.

We need to be honest, though. Most narcissists are not looking for help in the form of "light of awareness". Narcissists prefer we join them in the dark.

Furthering our motivation, we do not want others to suffer for the narcissist's chaos, so we step in as a buffer. I have played this role more times than I care to recount. Although inspired by kindness, acting in this manner costs a tremendous amount of time and energy. Your beautiful energy is used to transform the craziness resulting from the narcissist's need crazy-make.

Don't throw good energy in after bad. Value what you bring to a situation.

I choose to use my energy for things other than cleaning up the messes of others.

Yes! Absolutely, Yes!

Narcissists count on our willingness to explain away their crazy behavior.

As we witness narcissistic actions, a sense of denial may pervade our thinking. We simply do not want to believe any one could be so negative and hurtful. In reality, we are better served by simplicity and directness, rather than justifications and explanations.

Can a narcissist be this self-centered? Yes! Absolutely, Yes!

Can a narcissist have such little regard for others? Yes! Absolutely, Yes!

Can a narcissist lie consistently and blatantly to your face? Yes! Absolutely, Yes!

Even though you have court-worthy evidence showing the truth? Yes! Of course! ("Evidence" is relative to a narcissist.)

Can a narcissist show time and again that your needs don't matter? Yes! Absolutely, Yes! (Actually, what needs could you possibly have?)

Can a narcissist act as if everything is totally your fault? Yes! Absolutely, Yes!
Always? Yes! (...and forever)

Can a narcissist take your money and feel as if it were theirs for the taking anyway? Yes! Absolutely, Yes! (What is yours is theirs.)

The simple answer to whether the narcissist will likely commit the most egregious of behaviors is simply "Yes! Absolutely, Yes!" Chant it in a circle, hum it as a mantra.

Don't be caught off guard when narcissists show their capabilities

I am honest in my assessment of the behaviors and actions of others.

The Devil is in the Context

To a narcissist, details and context are items to be manipulated.

One of the stresses that victims of narcissism experience is the lack of resonance from others when explaining the abuse. Comments, such as "Well…that does not sound that bad", may follow such attempts.

Of course, the situational details associated with a narcissist do not sound "that bad", because narcissists make everything look good on the surface. Your stress and confusion are not related to the details, because narcissists are great at manipulating these.

With a narcissist, the devil is not in the details, it's in the context. The details may "make sense" to others and appear "fine" on the surface. However, the contextual message is there for the narcissist's victims, not the innocent bystander. The clues are meant only for you.

For example, a narcissist, in front of others, may appear willing to help out at a school function. However, the narcissist's victims know the context. The specific phrases and gestures used by the narcissist to convey his displeasure. The narcissist's agreement to help at a school function is the detail. The context is the narcissist's anger at having to do so.

The context of narcissism is difficult to relate to those who have never lived with such a dynamic. The lack of awareness by others does not make your experience any less real. You know the narcissist and the narcissist manipulates on many levels, details and context included.

I understand both the details and the context of a situation. I do not need others to verify what I sense and observe.

The Exchange Rate

"All for me" and "none for you" are common phrases used by narcissists engaged in "sharing".

Every relationship involves an exchange of energy. In some relationships, the energy exchange is equal. Narcissists insist they also "share" in relationships. Being narcissists, however, their self-contrived definition of "sharing" is distorted.

Let's look at the things you are expected to "share" with a narcissist. (And by "share", the narcissist means those things you are supposed to give to him or her from this point forward.)

Your time, your energy, your schedule, your days, your hours, your minutes, your behaviors, your home, your finances, your beliefs, your emotions, your words, your truth, your hopes, your self-will

But even a narcissist does not escape the relational exchange of energy. In return for all the narcissist "borrows", they also "give". (And by "give", the narcissist means those items for which you are now responsible.) Here are the items you are now in charge of caring about-

The narcissist's happiness, the narcissist's well-being, the narcissist's self-image, and the narcissist's fulfillment.

If anything goes awry with the above items, it is your fault because you did not care enough.

In a relationship with a narcissist, the exchange rate is ten thousand to one - ten thousand units of your caring to one unit of the narcissist's "sharing".

My resources are full and complete. I can decide when and where I would like to share them.

Air Traffic Controller

Like an air traffic controller, narcissists attempt to control the movement patterns of all around them.

Narcissists frequently spend time and energy in what I refer to as "Air Traffic Controller" mode.

In this analogy, people are the planes moving across the narcissist's screen of control, as the narcissist directs their movements. In order to protect their image and hide their behaviors (rather than addressing these behaviors) narcissists "coordinate" (read, "control") the engagement patterns and interactions of people.

Narcissists divert flight patterns of potential engagements by creating distractions and disruptions. Narcissists may also "ground" a person by declaring "no contact" between this person and those close to the narcissist. Narcissists may also place people in holding patterns indefinitely. Never allowing them to land, but never allowing them to move on.

Narcissists view people in their lives as an air traffic controller views the flights on his or her screen - as objects to direct and control.

Remember, you and only you, direct your flight pattern through life.

I am free to engage with others as I desire.

A Being without Compromise

Narcissists exist for conflict, not resolution.

Conflict is inevitable in the best of relationships. In a relationship with a narcissist, conflict is the status quo. In typical relationships, a number of strategies can be employed when conflicts arise, such as a cooling off period, discussions, and compromise.

Unfortunately, few of these apply to conflict resolution with a narcissist.

In every conflict, the narcissist has one approach to resolution-
"In it to win it."

If you look for compromise and a win-win solution with a narcissist, you have already lost. Narcissists don't do compromise and they do not understand win-win.

You give up things for the overall good of the relationship. The narcissist will not.

Any victory you may have, any concession you gain in working towards compromise is viewed as a significant loss to the narcissist.

When in a conflict with a narcissist, determine what works best for you. Because, rest assured, the narcissist has given no thought to such matters.

Conflict resolution can come in all forms. I am open to receiving resolutions that support my highest purpose.

Editorial Assistant

Narcissists have a prescribed script for their lives. If you dare deviate from this script, you are written out of the entire production.

Being the symbolic editorial assistant to a narcissist is one of the most lonely, isolating roles you can have. No one else is on the same page as the narcissist, because the page the narcissist is on is not real.

Tiny editorial suggestions that the narcissist's self-perceived script may need a little tweaking always falls on deaf ears. There is nothing like the complete stonewalling of a narcissist when he does not want to hear something that he should change. Such information is quickly and efficiently disposed of in the symbolic trash as the narcissist explains, denies lies, diverts, and projects.

Why do we even try to get narcissists to be aware of the shortcomings of their scripts?

Subconsciously, you know the better functioning the narcissist is, the better your life is. So, you suggest a rewrite here and there.

But you also have your script, and I am most certain, your life script was never to be the editorial assistant to the life of another.

I am the central character in my own life script.

Demagnetizing your self

Narcissists stick you with their emotions.

To a narcissist, we are convenient surfaces for the displacement and projection of their feelings and emotions. Narcissists can not be with their emotions in an authentic manner. They are often completely unaware or overwhelmed by their own feelings.

A narcissist and his or her own feelings are like the alignment of matching poles on two magnets. The result is immediate repulsion. This is where you come in. The narcissist's feelings exist and have to go somewhere. That "somewhere" is often you.

You become the attracting repository for the feelings the narcissist can not own. The feelings are not really yours, but rather the projections of the narcissist.

It is exhausting trying to handle the emotions of another. Thus, you need to "demagnetize" yourself.

Do not attract the narcissist's emotions towards you. Do not offer to help, explain, or manage the narcissist's feeling for him or her.

Kindly redirect the emotional energy of the narcissist back to where it belongs- with the narcissist.

My energetic surface is clean and clear. I do not attract, nor do I allow, the feelings and emotions of others to stick to me.

Fill in the Blank

When it comes to describing others, narcissists are generalists.

Growing up, we played a game in which one person had a written narrative with blanks throughout. The other person, unable to see the written narrative, would provide a noun or verb or whatever was needed to fill in the blanks. As you had no narrative context for the words you provided, crazy stories emerged, much to our amusement.

This game is an excellent example of how narcissists regard others. Rather than supplying generic nouns and verbs, narcissists supply vulgar words and insults with no relation to context. If you stop to pay attention, you find the narcissistic version produces narratives that are just as ridiculous and ungrounded as the stories we participated in during childhood.

Narcissists banter about labels such as "slut", "stupid", and "moron". It's the narcissistic version of "insert a word". If you are the target for the moment, they fill in your name and any and all harmful words into the blanks.

Although these labels may be irrelevant, it does not mean they cause no damage. We can sometimes get caught up in the narcissist's narrative and begin to question if we are "stupid" or "fat" or "ugly" or whatever term the narcissist has used.

Find better things to do with your time than counteract these made-up labels. Narcissists play this ridiculous game because it has worked for them in the past. They believe it shows they are better than others. What it actually shows is that they are children playing a childhood game.

I do not allow others to define and label me.

Will-Full Mal Intent

One word, "intentional", describes a narcissist's array of harmful behaviors.

The word to keep in mind when observing a narcissist's behavior is the word "intentional".

The narcissist "forgets" something important to you. It's intentional.

The narcissist "mistakenly" ignores you. It's intentional.

The narcissist "unknowingly" creates a chaotic situation. It's intentional.

The narcissist "unwittingly" neglects responsibility and blames you. It's intentional.

The narcissist "overlooks" saying thank you for a gift. It's intentional.

The narcissist "accidentally" destroys something of value to you. It's intentional.

It's intentional. It's intentional.

"It's intentional" should be your mantra.

It gets you out of the fantasy of trying to justify and understand the narcissistic behaviors.

Call the behaviors what they are – intentional acts to hurt you.

I make no excuses for the harmful behaviors of others.

Change-Less

Narcissists have little capacity to change, thus, they are surprised when others do.

Dear Narcissist,

I am tired of your "elastic" view of time. Things that happened years ago, you throw around as if they occurred yesterday.   "Never forgive and always retain" is your motto for the failures of others.

Your own transgressions, of course, are immediately forgotten and never remembered. In your mind, a reason always exists as to why you acted as you did. Thus, you have never once transgressed another.

I am sick of your self-serving, condescending words and gestures that "explain" your behaviors. We have a word for these whimsical tales. The word is "lies".

I am tired of your meandering, exploitive comments and conversations. The convoluted stories you create in regards to the persons, places, and objects that have "wronged" you have taken up my years.

In my exhaustion and confusion, something has become clear.

Many of us work with hope and optimism, trusting in our potential to change for the better. You, though, are stuck with you, and that, dear narcissist, must be the thought that makes you most sick and tired.

You work so hard to change those around you, sensing they have the gift- the one you never will - the ability to change

I am always changing for the better, and thus, so is my life.

Holiday Fear

Visions of chaos dance in their heads, while narcissists lay in bed, wondering how to become the reason for the season.

Holidays, or any special events, are commonly viewed as times to gather and share good cheer. Too often, though, when a narcissist is involved, holiday cheer turns to holiday fear.

Narcissists and holidays are never a good mix. Holidays push a narcissist into feeling a loss of control and power. When they sense a loss of power, narcissists become even more awkward and erratic when compared to normal.

The time and energy required to manage the narcissist increase several-fold during holidays. Secret discussions may occur around the narcissist. Where should the narcissist sit? What is a strategy for handling a narcissistic outbreak? Who is going to be the target of the narcissist's rage this time?

We get so caught up in managing the narcissist; we see this expenditure of energy as typical. The energy to manage the narcissist may be necessary, but that does not mean it costs you any less.

Nor does this sense of necessity lessen the pain and sadness that stain your memories of special events ruined by narcissistic behavior. It can be painful to see others happy and excited about holidays, while you feel a pit of dread in your stomach, because you worry about what the narcissist will do.

Holidays may be different for you with a narcissist in your life. However, give yourself permission to enjoy holidays and special occasions.

Don't let a narcissist consume YOUR reason for the season.

I determine the joy in my life. Joy meets me on my terms.

Fake It...Until You Don't?

Narcissists fake a lot of things, until at some point they can't even bother to fake it any more.

"Fake it until you make it."

Narcissists spend a lot of time living out this phrase, except they seldom reach the "make it" point.

Narcissists are all about faking it and creating a façade. That is, until the narcissist is suddenly "done".

No one knows why this sudden turn of events. Normally, the narcissist desires to keep up a good façade. But, at some point, the narcissist feels even putting up a false front is too much effort.

Does this cause the narcissist to worry that without the façade, he or she may be exposed? No, not at all.

The energy for maintaining the narcissist's superior image then falls to you.

Despite the narcissist quitting and no longer trying to maintain the facade, you are to act as if the narcissist is wonderfully and fully engaged.

If someone were to point out that the narcissist has quit and the facade is in a bit of disarray, he is confronted with the narcissist's rage. How dare anyone point out the shortcomings of the narcissist, even when the narcissist has quit?

Façade maintenance is now put upon all bystanders, who are expected to not fake it, but rather make it.

Life is real. I do not participate in the facades of others.

Reference Point

For narcissists, all roads lead to them.

The ability to incorporate a number of reference points into one's life is a sign of maturity. Books, friends, and therapy are all valuable points of reference to help us navigate our journeys.

Unfortunately, as is consistent with their patterning, narcissists never grow to psychological adulthood. Instead they see life as the children they are, with a reference point of one- "Me".

Narcissists have limited ability to integrate the ideas and experiences of others. To them, the world orbits from one axis- their personal views. As you can imagine, this personal axis is a bit wobbly.

As you crisscross the symbolic miles with the narcissist, you realize it is a journey with no final destination. The only stops along the way are those that can contribute to the narcissist's sense of self.

When a person becomes lost, the number one recommendation is for that person to stay put. This advice serves us well when a narcissist, using his or her internal compass, is guiding our travels.

If confronted with a directional change set by the narcissist, stop. Stay where you are and get your own bearings, before heading out in a different direction.

My life journey is guided by me.

Emotional T Rex

Narcissists are emotional <u>Tyrannosaurus rexes.</u>

Narcissists carry around a great deal of symbolic mass and weight. If they are in a room, you know it. If they want something, you know it. If they are displeased, you know it. If they are unhappy you know it. Why? Because the narcissist makes sure to show it.

Narcissists are not known for subtle, graceful movements. They rage, they stomp, they throw things, they lash out, and they hit. Narcissists count on everyone being fearful of their massive rages. They move through life, emotionally, like a *Tyrannosaurus rex* on the hunt.

But, there is always a cost to how we act and for all their symbolic mass, narcissists lack the one thing so many of us have- the ability to embrace life.

As much as their rage is overdeveloped, their hearts are underdeveloped.

Narcissists are like *T. rexes*, stomping, raging and creating destruction, all the while having teeny, tiny, little ineffective arms incapable of embracing the world.

The next time you see a narcissist roaring and stomping around, think of a *T. rex.* Yes, the beast is big, but you have it beat in your ability to hold the world close to your heart.

My capacity for love and kindness is infinitely wide. I use these gifts with wisdom.

Trump Card

Narcissists work very hard to stack the deck in their favor.

If we are to engage with a narcissist, we must do so from a point of awareness.

Awareness always trumps craziness.

Awareness is our trump card for cutting through all the narcissistic chaos.

We may want things to be different with the narcissist. We may hope he or she eventually heals. We may long to show them how life can be fun and joyous. But living in a world of light and love does not absolve us from the responsibility of being aware and protecting ourselves.

We can not always control and change everything to our liking, of course. Often, it is not our place to do so.

But, what we can do is always observe with awareness.

Awareness is our exit path out of confusion and into choices.

Awareness is my trump card.

Got Your Back…Never

Narcissists sacrifice anyone and everyone in order to keep from going under.

Narcissists invest very little in protecting their loved ones. The only back a narcissist "has", or covers, is his or her own. When the waters of life get deep, the narcissist pushes others down and stands on their shoulders to keep his own head above water.

Your survival or the narcissist's?

It's never a choice to the narcissist. You are simply an extension of the narcissist. If you have to be sacrificed in order for the narcissist to survive, then so be it, in the narcissist's mind.

If you are not aware of this dynamic, you can be surprised that the narcissist's first instinct is not to protect you.

Be aware that you can never feel protected if you are relying on a narcissist. Narcissists work to INCREASE your sense of vulnerability, not lessen it.

The protective detail for your life is you.

My survival is dependent on my actions and awareness. I put my own safety above the needs of others.

The "Parent" Trap

Narcissists attempting to parent are really children "raising" children.

Having never grown up themselves, narcissists are incapable of effectively parenting their children. Narcissists play-act at parenting, as they play-act at so many things, in order to get their own needs fulfilled, not the child's.

Narcissistic parenting becomes a collection of what a narcissist can not do, rather than what the narcissist can do.

Narcissists can not effectively love their children.
Narcissists are unable to see anything beyond self and this applies to their children. Any child of a narcissist is simply an extension of the narcissist, and thus, under narcissistic control.

Narcissists can not appropriately discipline their children.
Behaviors that should be reprimanded are instead encouraged or ignored. Behaviors that are part of a child being his or her own person are attacked and punished.

Narcissists can not effectively relate to their children.
The child serves as an extended projection of the narcissist. There is no one for the narcissist to relate to- other than his or her own sense of self.

Narcissists can not take care of the needs of their children.
The narcissist has no ability to recognize, let alone relate to and meet, the emotional or social needs of a child.

Narcissist can not play with their children.
Narcissists play-act all their roles in life. When you play-act as a parent, you have not space to really be a parent.

Children do not need parents who play-act at being an adult.

The Detachment Attachment

The slippery sides of a narcissist's personality make it difficult for us to attach.

Having had a relationship with a narcissist, we may confront a sense of difficulty in letting go. In some ways, we look over our time with the narcissist, and we see that the relationship was not healthy for us. So, why is it challenging to move on?

We find ourselves caught in the "detachment attachment" conundrum.

It is difficult to detach from someone that you felt *committed* to, but never felt *attached* to.

You sought attachment and companionship. Yet, when you reached for the narcissist, you were met with emptiness. The emptiness kept you reaching for more.

You can never truly be attached to a narcissist, though. The narcissist presents such a fake, unreal persona, nothing of solidity exists between the two of you. Thus, you struggle to let go of what you never had.

The way out of the "detachment attachment" conundrum is to stop seeking. Understand that what you seek can never be given to you by a narcissist. Pull back on reaching outwards and return the energy to yourself, where it can find something real with which to engage.

I seek commitment and attachment in my relationships.

Ceremonially Authentic

Narcissists are all about pomp, circumstance and ceremony, believing as they do that these compensate for authenticity.

Narcissists love carrying the bearing of the Grand Poobah of Life, and they believe they wear it quite well. What narcissists overplay in ceremony, though, they completely lack in authenticity.

Narcissists often dress the ceremonial part, and sometimes you can witness a complete change in behavior and physical bearing when narcissists are in ceremony mode. Like actors upon the stage, they embrace their roles. You are left as an astounded "audience member" as you witness this transformation. Everyone else, including you, is, of course, treated as a stage hand by the narcissist.

I have witnessed one narcissist who loves the ceremonial interactions of having a child in school. She plays the role of concerned parent, with a bit of superiority thrown into the mix. Yet, when it comes to the authentic acts of parenting a child in school- filling out reading logs, checking homework status, filling out paperwork- she is nowhere to be found. She has played her role. In her mind, what more can you expect her to do?

When you see a narcissist in performance mode, let them have their moment. Their performance eventually falls flat, as the world resonates with authenticity, not those who play-act.

In time, the narcissist's performance is met with the audience response it deserves- dead silence.

I am seeking an authentic life, not ceremonial posturing.

Where is karma when you need it?

Given the karmic debt narcissists accrue, you almost expect a tree to fall upon them at any moment.

I admit that in moments of confusion and anger, I have harbored ill wishes towards narcissists. When I witness narcissistic harmful acts, my first thought is "How dare they?" quickly followed by, "How can they get away with this?" I want someone (the narcissists) to have to pay for what they did. I want them to suffer in equal measure to the pain they cause.

At one time, I was caught in the fantasy that narcissists cause pain and harm to others, and then walk away to live happily ever after. The karmic wheel, though, spins in a multitude of directions, and what appears on the surface may only be an illusion.

If you stop to think about it, how many narcissists do you know that are living happily ever after? None. There is no "happily ever after" in narcissist land. Narcissists are not happy- ever. They are not joyous. They are not content.

They live in fear and anger, and this is the karmic debt for their transgressions. Joy is impossible for those set on harming others.

Living freely with joy is one of the fears of narcissists, and they believe if they can't have it, no one can. But, we rise above such ploys, and know joy and happiness are ours for the taking.

So although a tree may not fall upon the heads of narcissists, narcissists pay a steep karmic price, knowing "happily ever after" is not in their story.

I focus on my life and my happiness. I rise above games designed to entrap me in turmoil.

Keep your Hands and Hopes out of the Cage

A quiet, patient narcissist may be the most dangerous type.

At some point, you get smart and build a cage around the narcissist. You draw your lines and erect your boundaries. The narcissist no longer has access to your life, because you made it that way. For good measure, you may even symbolically electrify the bars of the cage.

Then…wait…what is this?

The narcissists appear to respond to your signals. After all these years and all this time, they are seemingly nicer and kinder. Can you dare hope? No. You can not.

Do you really think narcissists will continue to fling themselves against the bars of your cage? No. Remember, to a narcissist, survival is paramount, self-sacrifice is not.

The narcissists have changed strategies. Outwardly, they appear calm. They pretend to sit in the cage of your made-up boundaries and rules, and act like they want to play nice, very nice.

But in reality, they sit in the cage of your making with only one thought in mind- "How in the hell do I get out of here and who is going to pay when I do?"

When you are finally strong enough to set boundaries with a narcissist, be smart enough to keep your hands and your hopes out of the cage. You put the bars and your boundaries there for a reason. If you don't honor these, the narcissist never will.

I create boundaries for a sound reason- I am valuable enough to protect.

The Dictionary of Narcissists

Narcissism is a state in which words have no meaning.

The dictionary of narcissists is approximately one page in length, with a single entry.

ANY word:
ANY meaning currently assigned by the narcissist
that meets his or her needs in the moment

This is the complete dictionary.

Words that have clear meaning to everyone else are twisted and contorted by the narcissist until the words lose all meaning. If you attempt to point out this confusing mess, the narcissist attacks you for being too dumb to understand their "simple" explanations.

As narcissists craft one delusional explanation after another, they create verbal tornadoes that leave you feeling dizzy. You know how frustrating it is to go around and around on issues with narcissists, as they banter about their unique, strange meanings of words.

Narcissists are always explaining what they "meant" and how you "misunderstood" what they said. Narcissists use words for one purpose-to support their illusions.

You know what words mean, and more importantly, you understand the actions you see. Don't get caught up in the dictionary of the narcissist.

I trust in my understanding of the meaning of words and context. I do not need to be told meaning by others.

Off the Hook

Narcissists use YOUR concern about THEIR feelings to keep you on the relationship hook.

Narcissists employ many strategies to keep us engaged and worried about their lives and well-being. I refer to this as "being on the hook" with a narcissist. Narcissists bait us with their drama, their neediness, and their play upon our compassion and empathy.

Because narcissists do not like to expend a lot of energy getting their needs met, they often, at first, just drop a lure in our psyche. They hint around. They provide slight mental/emotional nudges.

If we don't snap up the symbolic lure, the narcissist ups the attractiveness of the bait. They become friendly and nice (or their version of it). They butter us up with flattery. They get us to focus on their emotional state- how upset they are, how they miss us, how hurt and damaged they are by life, and so on. They use our feelings to hook us. As soon as we bite, the narcissist reels us in, and we find ourselves knee-deep in their messes and emotional drama.

What we must do, and this goes against most of our natures, is IGNORE the narcissist's feelings.

When we see someone upset (and God forbid if we feel we have a hand in upsetting someone), we want to make things better, and this is where we get caught with the narcissist. To get yourself off the narcissist's hook (or to never get on it in the first place) you must stop worrying about how the narcissist feels and pay more attention to how you feel.

I pay attention to my feelings before worrying about the feelings of others.

The Inversion Layer

Narcissists view themselves as priority number one, in their lives and yours.

Because narcissists are unable to be aware of others and the needs of others, the narcissist's priorities and agenda for the day center on the following- 1. What is my first need? 2. What is my second need? 3. Who can I get to meet these needs?

Narcissists, simply by being narcissists, already take up an inordinate amount of time. They can't help it. A trip to the doctor for a minor sinus infection by these types can end up taking hours of YOUR day.

If you allow the narcissist to drive the agenda of your interactions, you find your priority list constantly inverted- with the narcissist always ending up in position number one.

You can not allow the narcissist to occupy this coveted position mentally, physically, or emotionally.

Narcissists constantly try to invert the priority lists of others, by placing their needs and demands near the top of everyone's life. They often create this inversion by crafting some type of drama to grab attention and send everyone into crisis mode. Don't buy into such behaviors.

You control the agenda and priorities of your life not the narcissist.

Where I invest my time and energy each day is up to me.

Surprise!

Narcissists count on YOUR predictability.

Narcissists love to use the element of surprise to harm others. They just don't like being surprised themselves. An element of abuse that keeps our stress level high is that we do not know when the next attack may come.

Narcissists are especially adept at keeping us engaged by keeping us off-guard. These "surprises" are designed to do one thing- keep your attention on the narcissist.

But, two can play this game, and the element of surprise also applies to you. Although narcissists love to surprise others, they are banking on you being predictable. In fact, one way narcissists attempt to control is by predicting everyone else's behaviors. Thus, surprising the narcissist is one of your greatest powers.

If you normally confront on a certain issue, for a day, decide to ignore it. If you normally ignore, throw a fit. If you normally attempt to placate everyone, become demanding.

Narcissists are so used to getting their own way, they suck at adapting. Put the burden of surprise on them and move on with your day.

I am free from old, repetitive patterns.

Problem "Solving"

A narcissist solving a problem is like the surgeon who declares, "The operation was a success, but the patient died."

In the course of each of our lives, we all have problems. We lean on one another during these times, gaining wisdom and insights. Most of us want to help one another in this way.

A narcissist, at times, displays some interest in solving your problems. The reason for this is simple- your problems take away from the narcissist's life and issues. What is a narcissist to do if you are wrapped up in problems that pertain to you? This scenario motivates the narcissist to attempt to "solve" your problems, so everyone can move on to the real issue at hand, the suffering and drama of the narcissist.

I witnessed this play out in an interaction between a narcissist and a child. The narcissist was presented with clear details of a significant problem. The issue had been occurring for years and appeared to be worsening.

The narcissist stepped forward to provide "help" in a way that only a true narcissist can- by denying the problem. The narcissist's response was simple, "You are fine. I have fixed it." Huh? What exactly is "fine" for a child who has been suffering for years? What exactly does "fix it" mean in relation to a problem getting larger not smaller?

Can you imagine the narcissist's response had this treatment been turned on her? The rage the narcissist would feel would be limitless. How dare anyone belittle any issue important to a narcissist? Yet, a narcissist does this to others- ALL the time.

I seek help and support only from those willing and capable of giving it.

Translation

Narcissists manage to be at once obviously and covertly subversive.

Interacting with a narcissist almost requires a behavior translator. For example, a narcissist may suddenly become involved in an ongoing issue. The narcissist sees his message as, "Look at me. I am so concerned." Others translate this as, "Why is he getting involved now? He never did before."

When narcissists jump into handle something, already handled by another, the narcissist thinks, "Sigh...MUST I handle everything? No one can do anything without me." Others see the narcissist as controlling and over-stepping.

If you do not immediately applaud the narcissist's sudden engagement, the narcissist believes, "Sigh...Everyone is such a failure. People can't even bother to notice my efforts." Others are actually too busy living and participating in life to notice the narcissist's fantasy.

When the narcissist suddenly stops engaging, the narcissist thinks, "My work is done here. I have more important things to do." Others have the correct interpretation. When the narcissist stops engaging, it is because the narcissist is no longer getting attention.

As you can see, with narcissists, if you know how to translate their behaviors, their covert attempts to manipulate situations and people are quite obvious.

With time, we all see behind the narcissist's disguise.

I note when the intentions and actions of others do not align.

Watch the Follow Through

Narcissists don't tip their hand with the first card they show.

How do you know a narcissist is telling lies? It's not the initial lie itself. We believe what people tell us, because we know most people have no reason to lie. So, when the narcissist tells us something, our first instinct is to trust. And let's be honest, most of us are much too busy to seek confirmation of each and every thing the narcissist says, so we operate on faith.

Over time, though, narcissists reveal their own lies – by missing the follow through.

For example, let's say, the narcissist creates a big, convoluted story about a success at work. When you ask, "What did your coworker say about that project?" The narcissist stumbles. Their follow through is off and they have no believable response.

Usually, the narcissist has not thought far enough ahead to create follow through actions that match their original statement. What is "real" to narcissists is whatever they make up in their heads, so they don't plan a follow through to the lie. We often catch a narcissist in a lie, well after the initial lie, when we see it in the follow through.

Don't let the timing of your discovery of the truth prohibit you from honoring the truth. One trick of narcissists, when you catch them in a lie, is to try to turn the tables on you. They insist that since you believed the initial lie that you must support it.

Information comes to us in all different forms and all different times. Honor the information whenever you receive it.

I take information whenever I receive it. I am not held to the timeline of another.

Re-entry Phenomenon

Narcissists are in a constant state of free fall.

Because narcissists travel in fantastical, self-created orbits, far, far away from reality, when they are confronted with reality, it can be very disconcerting for them. The narcissists are all happy, floating around in their delusional orbit- and then WHAM! Some thing or someone derails the orbit.

I call this "Narcissistic Re-entry Phenomenon".

Normally, this occurs only when narcissists have to interact with anyone outside their sphere of control. Narcissists are very good at keeping their orbits from plummeting into free fall by exerting complete control on everyone around them.

However, like all of us, the narcissist's orbital path eventually bumps up against something or someone outside his or her control. Situations and people include: teachers, school principals, waiters, waitresses, baristas, doctors, attorneys, judges, grocery store clerks, receptionists and so on.

Anyone or anything that does not get in line with the narcissist's orbital trajectory (i.e. follow each and every command) is likely to stimulate re-entry phenomenon in the narcissist. Symbolic pieces go flying everywhere as the narcissist's control falls apart.

It is important to note how this may impact you. Your stress level likely increases when you sense the narcissist is forced to deal with reality. You worry how bad the re-entry will be. Will the narcissist begin screaming at everyone? Threatening people? Be completely clueless?

At the end of the day, you are not responsible for the narcissist's re-entry into reality. It's a price they pay for living in a fantasy orbit.

I do not need to manage the decisions and consequences of others.

The Unholiest of Exchanges

To a narcissist, everything, including love, is a commodity not to be shared.

Narcissists demand so much love and attention and give so little in return. When we experience this lack of return of our love, we fall into the trap of the unholiest of exchanges- we give and give in order to get.

Dealing with a narcissist can set into motion a perpetual sense of "I am not enough", " I must do more and give more", "If I were a better person, then I would receive the love I desire" and so on.

When we are in pain, we long to get out of pain. So, our mind begins to craft stories and ways of lessening our pain. We believe if we give more to the narcissist, eventually, surely, the narcissist will feel fulfilled and loved, and return love to us. This type of thinking is like stepping onto a treadmill of insanity.

The problem is not with your giving. The problem is with the narcissist's personality and interpersonal skills. The pull you feel to give love to the narcissist is intentionally created by the narcissist. The narcissist wants you to feel pain, so that you return to the narcissist to ease your pain. Don't do it.

Narcissists are empty, thus, have nothing to give. Save your time and resources for those who understand the holy, sacred nature of relationships- the exchange of giving.

My relationships are fulfilling, with an equal exchange of love.

Isolation

Both physical and mental isolation occur at the hand of the narcissist.

Narcissists live on their own, man-made island of fantasy, far from the shores of others. When you relate to a narcissist, you and all others under the narcissist's control, become the sole inhabitants of this island.

Most are aware of the physical isolation brought on by abuse and the abuser.

However, I think often times the mental isolation is overlooked.

Unless you live it, no one understands the bizarre, convoluted world the narcissist creates. The more you are around the narcissist, the more time you have to spend on his or her mental/emotional island.

Thus, you become isolated not only physically, but also mentally, because no one else is living with you on this island of make-believe.

Any symbolic attempts to have flights of Truth and Reality land on this island are subsequently shot down.

My Being fosters union not isolation.

To and Fro

Narcissists float to and fro on the same issue- even an issue they created.

If one day, a narcissist requires your engagement and assurance that something is "white", don't be surprised if the narcissist appears the next day asserting the object is to now "black". Narcissists are not internally stable, thus their thoughts and expressions are not stable.

Interacting with a narcissist is to live a pendulum-like experience. We sprint in one direction to keep up with the narcissist, only to have to reverse course as he or she swings in the other direction.

But, don't be fooled.

As narcissists swing to and fro on issues, they are the ones clinging to the symbolic pendulum. Narcissists get caught in the momentum of their own declarations.

In this case, the cart is driving the horse. The narcissists are being taken for a ride by their own delusions. You don't have to ride along with them.

Before committing to the ideas of others, I take a moment to reflect on my own needs.

Checkmate- Your Move!

Narcissists hate to be forced into a move.

Sometimes when dealing with a narcissist, the best move is no move.

Narcissists hate being held responsible for anything. They prefer to hide in the shadows, controlling the "puppets" of their lives. A good strategy with a narcissist, then, is to force the narcissist to take responsibility by making a decision.

Think of playing a game of chess. At times, after your opponent's play, you do not want to make the next move, because as you scan the board, you realize you have no good move. Any move you make costs you.

Life also follows this format. We don't get to make our plays in life and then blame everyone else. Nor do we get to "skip a turn" when we know a decision is going to cost us. Sometimes tough moves need to be made.

Try this strategy with a narcissist. Sit back and refuse to do anything basically saying, "It's your move". Do not jump in and help the narcissist or rearrange the symbolic game pieces for the narcissist.

Sit and sit and sit, clearly indicating you will not budge until the narcissist makes his or her move. Will the narcissist be annoyed with you?

Of course. But you play by the rules and the fact the narcissist does not is not your problem. Game on.

I am patient.

Soul Warrior

Narcissists push and then push some more.

When a soul is pushed to a certain point, the soul goes to war.

I think many of us who have narcissists in our life can relate to this statement.

When we look back on our interactions with a narcissist, we may be surprised at the things we have said or the actions we have taken.

At times we may judge ourselves for being "mean" or "petty" for treating someone, even those who have wounded us with their narcissistic behaviors, in this manner.

But, what I have realized is that although such behaviors may not reflect our "best", pushing back against a narcissist is needed.

When we put forth strong behaviors to protect ourselves, we show that we believe we are of value. A soul which fights back is a soul showing it believes in its own worth.

I am a warrior for the integrity and honoring of my Soul and its purpose.

Swimming Upstream

Narcissism is a long, lonely journey, traveling upstream against the principles of the Universe.

I believe there are certain principles to life.

When we are in alignment with these principles, a sense of comfort and hope prevails.

For those who have suffered narcissistic abuse, however, the messages received are training against these principles.

Where the Universe works on love, you learned fear.
Where the Universe works on freedom, you learned bondage.
Where the Universe works on hope, you learned fearful anticipation.
Where the Universe works on rhythm, you learned discord.
Where the Universe works on truth, you learned denial.
Where the Universe works on continuity, you learned chaos.
Where the Universe works on creativity, you learned destruction.
Where the Universe works on encouragement, you learned belittlement.
Where the Universe works on empathy, you learned cruelty.
Where the Universe works on trust, you learned second-guessing.
Where the Universe works on balance, you learned extremism.

For all this time, you have been swimming upstream of how the Universe works.

I trust in the Universal principles to support me. I do not work against those things I know to be true.

The Blame Game

Narcissists count on you blaming yourself before you blame them.

Narcissists leave their mark, perhaps not always physically, but certainly, always emotionally. Sometimes, though, we fail to hold the narcissist accountable for his or her actions.

We fall into the trap of blaming ourselves for what the narcissist has done. We see what the narcissist has done is wrong, yet we blame ourselves for being the "victim" of the narcissist's behaviors. We may not acknowledge the actions of the narcissist or how we have suffered, because we do not want to blame anyone. We don't want to be the victim any longer, and we long to take responsibility for our own lives.

We transpose the idea of self-responsibility, however, into something it was never meant to be. We are always being asked to be aware, and sometimes awareness leads us to an understanding of what has been done to us. This is called acknowledgment, not blaming.

When we fear blaming others, we lose our own awareness in the process. We are each responsible for our own lives, and that includes the narcissist. When the narcissist has hurt and harmed you, you are not blaming anyone by calling out these behaviors.

You are taking responsibility for your experiences in your honest awareness of them.

I can blame or not blame, but I will always acknowledge my experiences.

Eyes Wide Open

The one gaze a narcissist can not stand is an all-knowing witness.

Narcissists lie, cheat, blame and shame you, all in the hopes of keeping you in the dark about how mean, cruel, and destructive narcissists are.

Given enough time, though, you begin to see through the narcissist.

Once you begin seeing, you can't stop seeing.

You see through the narcissist's sleight of hand (or sleight of mind) tricks. Of course, your found vision will not make the narcissist happy.

Despite spending hours symbolically gazing at their own reflections, narcissists can not stand to be truly seen by the eyes of another.

The paradox of narcissists is that you are never to let them out of your vision, but, on the other hand, you are never to truly see them.

I see the truth before me.

Take a Vacation for the Psyche

Narcissists never take a break from being narcissistic.

Narcissists long to consume you and your entire life- and they will, if you let them. Thus, you need to take conscious mini-vacations from the narcissist.

Mini-vacations, as the name implies, do not need to be substantial.

Leave the narcissist mentally for a bit. The narcissist can continue talking and talking, but you don't need to be actively listening. Leave the room for a moment. Make up an excuse and scurry somewhere less draining.

Make scheduling conflicts work to your advantage. Can you help it if you are always double-booked with other commitments, just when the narcissist needs you the most?

Have a buffer with you when you deal with the narcissist. Not that you want to expose others to the narcissist's craziness, but having someone along with you can help lessen the load of being the narcissist's sole focus.

Plan exit routes from phone or in-person conversations. Know what you are getting into and how you can get out of it.

Give yourself the break you need, because the narcissist never will.

Rest and relaxation are valuable parts of my life.

Management Crisis

Narcissists can't manage themselves, so they expect you to do it for them.

It's very difficult to change things of which we are consciously aware (think, smoking). Changing something of which we are not consciously aware is next to impossible.

Narcissists are not consciously aware of their narcissism, how could they be? They lack the introspection to do so. Plus, for narcissists, so many of their behaviors work to their benefit, the motivation to change is limited.

I am embarrassed to admit, though, that in the past none of these insights stopped me from trying to help the narcissist change.

In regards to one narcissist, I had the following set of thoughts - "He needs my help. I am aware of his unconscious drives. He had a bad childhood. He feels unloved. Let me show him true love and this will stop his abuse."

Too many people fall for the idea that they can somehow change the narcissist or at least stop the narcissistic abuse. We spin this fantasy to make ourselves feel better. We want to believe we can change narcissism, as the idea plays to our sense of hope and purpose. The narcissist participates in this fantasy, as well, gladly pushing all responsibility for their behavior onto us.

When this happens, you are in management crisis mode. The narcissist can't manage him or herself, and you can't manage him or her, either. Left on its own, this loop plays endlessly- the narcissist never responsible and you being over-responsible.

You have no one to manage but yourself, and that is enough.

My management skills are best applied to my own life.

Out of Stock

Narcissists are forever trying to work out how to get a lifetime of narcissistic supply.

To sustain themselves, narcissists seek what has been termed as "narcissistic supply". If you have had a narcissist in your life, you have been a supplier, whether you are conscious of this or not.

When you do become aware that you are the supplier to the narcissist, you enter a realm of power. The narcissist needs you more than you need him or her.

Eventually, as the supplier, you decide to be "out of stock" of narcissistic supply. Perhaps you don't return a phone call. You may or may not remember a birthday or other important occasions. You may pay attention to a conversation with a narcissist or you may not.

You have what the narcissist wants and that is why he or she is so demanding. You get to choose though, when and if you give it.

Sometimes, you are run out of narcissistic supply with no desire to reorder.

I decide to whom I give my love and devotion.

Trained by the Best

Narcissists train you on their terms.

At some point, the tables turn on narcissists. Narcissists are so used to being in power and control, they often overlook when the power has begun to shift.

For so long, the narcissist views you as weak and compliant. Thus, he or she underestimates your internal strength built up over all the years of having to deal with the narcissist.

Over time, the internal strength you gained through trying to manage the narcissist comes back to haunt the narcissist.

After years of living or engaging with a narcissist, you have learned nothing if not the art of resilience. Why should the narcissist always be the recipient of your growth and successes? Why not use what you learned from surviving narcissism and turn it around and use it to support you- your goals, your dreams, and your hopes?

When the narcissist is shocked or dismayed or angry that you have stood up to him or her and are NOT backing down, you can simply turn and say,

"Don't be surprised. I have been trained by the best to survive."

I find my power in all situations.

End Game with your Narcissist

In the end, the narcissist does not matter. You do.

After spending so much purposeful time and energy on understanding ourselves and the relationship to the narcissist, we may feel the energy plateauing. We either remove the narcissist from our lives, or if unable to do that, we become more adept at handling the narcissist.

Still, though, we may be looking for something...we are just not sure what. At this point, a sense of confusion may emerge. After all the drama, fear, anger and upset caused by the narcissist, you expect some type of resolution.

We imagine a battle, words to be exchanged, an apology issued. We want to fight and express all that we underwent. We want some inkling of awareness on the narcissist's part about the damage caused.

We think about payback. We think about compensation. We believe in karma and make an altar to it. Basically, we want the culminating act to this drama.

We feel we lost so much in dealing with the narcissist; we somehow want those pieces returned to restore themselves. We want back our missing days and years.

The "end game" with a narcissist may not be the "end" we imagine. We are changed by the experience and we become something different than we imagined. We are wiser, more aware, but more cautious, too. We have replaced naiveté with awareness, soft boundaries with firm borders.

In the end, we come to understand that we have been resolute in our own restoration and perhaps that is the only "end game" that really matters.

My well-being is the "end game" I desire.

About the Author

Kimberly Harding is a college professor living in Colorado. She can be reached at kharding@coloradomtn.edu.